the SIMPLE SIMON GUIDE to
PATCHWORK QUILTING

Two Girls, Seven Blocks, 21 Blissful Patchwork Projects

liZ Evans • Elizabeth Evans

Fons&Porter
CINCINNATI, OHIO

CONTENTS

INTRODUCTION

As we began researching the origins of the quilt blocks included in this book, we discovered that they all either found their beginnings or rose to popularity during the early 1800s. We also discovered that it is widely accepted by historians that the women who raised quilting to an art form and a cherished tradition during this era did so simply to mark significant events in the lives of their loved ones: birth, coming of age, marriage, moving, childbearing and death. The blocks that have become so iconic with frontier life and American tradition were created for the sole purpose of showing love and that seemed all too familiar to us.

Both of us were raised in different homes on opposite sides of the country. However, we both come from a long line of quilters, crocheters and crafters; from women who also created handmade gifts to mark the significant events in our own lives. From hand-crocheted blessing gowns to handmade baby blankets to hand-stitched wedding quilts, we find with each new period in our lives the handiwork of the women who came before us is always there.

It has been said many times that quiltmaking history is really quiltmaking "herstory." Quilts show in remarkable detail the environment, conditions and ingenuity of the women who created them. The fabrics used give us clues about the economic status of these women and the supplies available to them. The patterns they chose to quilt tell us if they had the luxury of extra time in the evening for handiwork (as is evidenced by the intricate designs and embroidery of crazy quilts) or if time spent quilting was a luxury in and of itself (many frontier quilts were of the Nine Patch and Log Cabin variety). But whether the fabrics were the new prints of the day or scraps from tattered clothing, each quilt tells a beautiful story about love and the human spirit.

And it is not just quilts from the 1800s that tell such compelling stories—these histories continue to be shared. As we look back at our own cherished items from mothers, grandmothers and aunts, we recognize variations in supplies, styles and details that each tell their own personal stories. And we appreciate these objects all the more.

Quilting has always been a powerful art form. The 1800s were a time of great migration and women could only carry with them a precious few belongings. Not surprisingly, quilts were always among those possessions. Not only did quilts serve a practical purpose but they served possibly an even more important purpose, surrounding people with both much needed warmth on treks across an untamed frontier and with comfort, love and the memories of the women who cared for them most.

We believe that we need the art of quilting just as much today as we did in the 1800s, both for ourselves and for our children. We admire the talent, creativity and determination of the quilters who have come before us, and we hope to keep the tradition alive in our own homes and pass it on to others. We created this book in an effort to keep this grand tradition alive, and we sincerely hope you find it both helpful and informative.

— Elizabeth and liZ

Chapter One
TOOLS & TECHNIQUES

As you begin (or continue) to create patchwork quilts, you will quickly discover that not only do you have a set of favorite tools to work with but that you have favorite techniques, too. Because of this, we pulled together all of our favorite tools and the techniques in one place to help you get started.

In this chapter we will walk you through the processes that we use most often (like sewing, binding, basting and constructing quilt backs). We refer back to the methods outlined in this chapter often and hope that you will find them helpful.

We understand that there as many ways to make a quilt as there are quilt patterns. If, for instance, our method for adding sashing is different than the way your grandmother taught you, that's OK! Go with what you know! (Or be daring and try something new.) Either way will work. In quilting, there is no technique that can only be accomplished one way. Patchwork quilting is an art form and, as such, is made all the more beautiful by the individuality expressed not only in the pattern and fabric selections but in the methods of construction, as well. So, enjoy the process and feel free to experiment with the techniques.

TOOLS

While you don't need every tool on this list to make the projects in the book, there are a few basic tools.

Basic Sewing Tools

A rotary cutter, when paired with a rotary mat and quilting ruler, is one of the fastest and most accurate methods for cutting fabric. We'll go over how to use them in a bit.

Fabric scissors are a must. Make sure you don't use your fabric scissors to cut anything else (paper will dull them quickly).

You can use any type of straight pin to pin your pieces together before sewing. Take care to remove them as you're sewing: stitching over a pin can ruin your machine.

There are many different threads on the market. For the projects in this book, any all-purpose thread will work. Choose one in a color that coordinates with your project.

Always keep a seam ripper nearby. Mistakes are part of the process, and a seam ripper is a quick and relatively painless way to remove stitches.

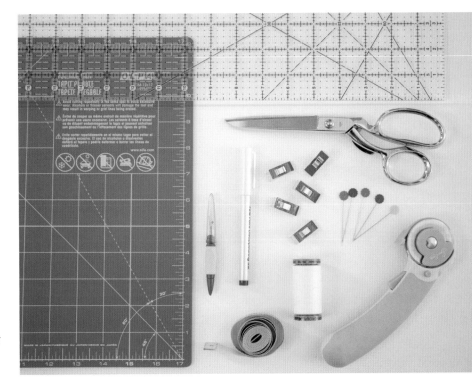

You'll need a removable fabric marker or fabric chalk for drawing stitching lines on your projects from time to time. If you plan on quilting any of your projects with your machine, you'll draw the quilting lines on first, then wash them away.

Sewing Machine Accessories

Aside from a trusty sewing machine, we recommend a few specialty sewing machine feet to help make sewing easier. A walking foot is great for doing the actual quilting on a project. A zipper foot is helpful when making the *Flying Geese Zipper Pouch*.

Nonessential Tools

You can certainly make do without these tools, but they are helpful. Wonder Clips are great when you need to hold multiple layers together, like a quilt top, batting and backing!

Since most of the projects in this book are sewn with a ¼" (6mm) seam allowance, having a ¼" (6mm) piecing foot for your sewing machine will help ensure accurate seam allowances.

Squaring-up rulers make squaring your blocks quick and easy. Look for both the Half-Square Triangle ruler and the Flying Geese ruler.

How to Cut Fabric

A cutting mat, quilting ruler and rotary cutter are very helpful for cutting fabric. We have found over the years that the more precisely you cut your fabric, the better the quilt turns out in the end. You will have less trimming to do and a more accurate quilt block. The easiest way to cut fabric is to cut it into strips and then cut your strips into individual squares. Here's how to do that:

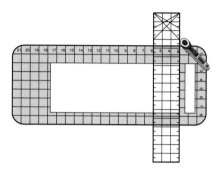

1 Lay the fabric on your cutting mat, aligning the edge of the fabric with a straight horizontal line. You may need to fold your fabric. Make sure the top and bottom of your fabric are on straight lines.

2 Place your quilting ruler on a straight vertical line according to the ruler on the mat. Make sure that the top and bottom of the ruler are aligning with the same number on the mat. Cut along that straight edge. This will give you a straight vertical line to start (called *squaring up the fabric*).

3 Keeping one hand firmly on the quilting ruler to keep it straight along the number line, run the rotary cutter along the edge of the quilting ruler to cut your strip of fabric.

4 Repeat steps 2 and 3 until you've cut all the strips you need for your project.

5 Once you have the right number of strips, you can subcut them into squares. Align a strip of fabric along a horizontal line on the cutting mat, making sure the top and bottom are straight. Use your quilting ruler to line up and square off your fabric, then cut the strip into squares (or rectangles).

How to Press Blocks

At Simple Simon we like to say that better pressing equals better quilting. And we really believe it. It's important to realize that pressing and ironing are not the same thing. Pressing involves lifting and lowering your iron onto the desired area, while ironing involves pushing your iron across the desired area. (When you press, it's lift, lower, press, lift, lower, press. When you iron, it's just a back and forth sliding motion.) Pressing is a combination of heat, pressure and steam that allows you to mold and shape your fabric. Here are some tips for better pressing:

1 Always press on the wrong side of the fabric. Pressing on the wrong side of the fabric allows you to properly see all the seams and therefore press them as crisply and correctly as possible.

2 Before pressing your seams open, always press them flat first. If you press your seams flat before pressing them open, you will be able to "set" the stitches into the fabric. It makes a crisper fold and will help eliminate puckers.

3 Never press over tape or pins. Pins will leave imprints and scratch your iron, while tape will melt and leave goo all over your iron and fabric.

4 Slide an envelope or piece of cardstock between your seam allowance and top fabric to avoid having your seam allowance press through and mark the front of your fabric.

5 Use the correct setting on your iron. If your iron is too cool, your pressing won't be sharp. If your iron is too hot, your iron may stick to the fabric or cause it to melt, pucker or even smoke! (We know all of this from sad, sad experience, especially with synthetic fabrics.) If you are unsure which setting to use, test it first on a scrap of the fabric you are planning to use and see how it reacts to your iron.

6 Iron all fabric before beginning any project (before you even start cutting). Yes, we said iron and not press. In this case, ironing is perfectly acceptable. Ironing at this stage will help ensure accurate cutting. Even if it may seem unnecessary, time-consuming or just a plain old pain, we promise it will be worth it in the end and will always help to give your project (whatever that may be) a more professional look.

How to Nest Your Seams

The term "nesting seams" simply means aligning the seams of each row so that they not only line up nicely but seem to almost fit together perfectly like a puzzle piece. This is done through a combination of pressing, pinning, and stitching.

The example below shows the directions seams are pressed, block by block, row by row in a Nine Patch quilt block.

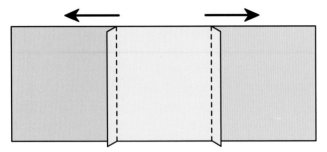

1 In row 1 of your block, the seams are pressed in opposite directions, away from the center block.

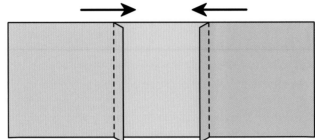

2 In row 2 of the block, the seams are both pressed in toward the center block.

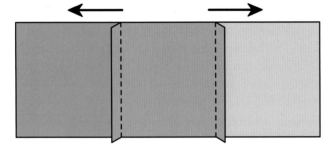

3 Row 3 is the same as row 1: the seams are pressed away from the center block.

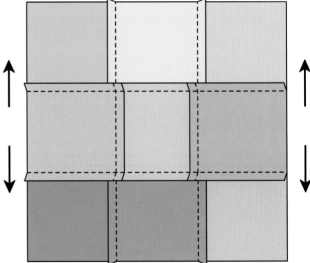

4 When joining the rows, again, alternate the direction of the pressed seams. Here, the row seams are both pressed away from the center row.

How to Add Borders and Sashing

Borders can be wide or narrow, patterned or plain. They help to really unify a quilt and show-case your quilt blocks. There are many methods for attaching borders but we have found that the easiest way is to first create border strips. Because borders are rather long, they need to be pieced together using strips of fabric that are the desired width of your border.

Once your border strip is pieced together, simply start pinning the borders onto the quilt one side at a time, right sides together. Sew them to the quilt using a ¼" (6mm) seam allowance. Finish them by pressing all the border seams in the same direction (either all toward the quilt center or all away from the quilt center).

Sashing is a fantastic way to both add a little more length and width to a quilt as well as really make your quilt blocks pop! Sashings are the strips of fabrics that many quilters add between each block. Like borders, sashing can be wide or narrow, patterned or plain, and can be added to your quilt using a wide variety of methods. When we add sashings, we simply treat them as another quilt block—a very plain, narrow quilt block.

To do this, pin your sashing to your quilt block with right sides together and sew using a ¼" (6mm) seam allowance. When finished, open and press the sashing all in the same direction (either all towards the quilt block or all away from the quilt block).

How to Square Up a Quilt Block

Squaring up a quilt block is another technique that can make a good quilt look great. We often skipped this step when we first started quilting, but taking those few extra minutes to square up (straighten up) your quilt blocks can make a big difference. Your quilt will appear more symmetri-cal, and the overall quilt will be more square and precise. We love to use square rulers (and a Fly-ing Geese ruler) to square up our blocks. We will demonstrate this on a Half-Square Triangle quilt block to show you how it is done.

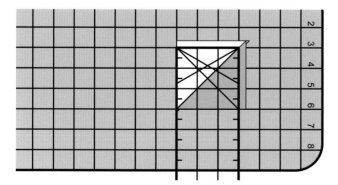

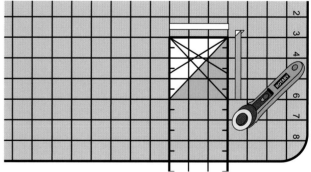

1 Lay your quilt block down under your clear ruler, placing the 45-degree angle (bias line) over the line where your two fabrics meet in your Half-Square Triangle block.

2 Now use your rotary cutter to trim off the scant edges that are hanging over the clear square ruler to fit the measurements of the quilt block in the pattern. Repeat for all 4 sides. Your quilt block is now squared up!

How to Assemble a Quilt Back

Quilt backs can be made in a variety of ways. The most important thing to remember is to make your quilt back larger than your quilt top. The back is made larger because sometimes during quilting, the quilt can shift a bit and you want to make sure the quilt back is large enough to accommodate any shifting. If you're sending your quilt to a long-arm quilter, be sure to ask for their specific measurements, but 3–4" (7.6–10.2cm) all the way around is a good standard measurement.

Because most of your quilts will be wider than 45" (114.3cm) (the average width of a bolt of fabric), you will need to piece together your quilt back. You can use two pieces of the same fabric for a simple quilt back, or you can use leftover fabrics to make a scrappy back for the quilt. Be creative and have just as much fun with the quilt back as you do with the quilt front!

How to Baste a Quilt

The term *baste* in quilting means to temporarily hold the three layers (the quilt top, the batting and the quilt backing) in place until the quilt can be quilted. There are several methods to baste a quilt, and we'll look at a few of them here.

In each method, the quilt back is laid down first on a smooth, hard surface with the right side of the fabric facing down. We like to use masking tape to hold this layer smooth and taut (but not stretched). The batting is placed on top of the quilt back and again pulled smooth and taut (but not stretched). The quilt top is then laid on top of the batting (right-side up) to complete the three layers of the quilt. In quilting, this method is some-times also referred to as "the quilt sandwich."

Keep in mind if you are sending your quilt to a long-arm quilter or someone who will quilt the quilt for you, you DO NOT need to baste your quilt. This process will be done by the person who is quilting and usually involves quilt frames to baste it together. Use the following basting methods only if you plan to quilt your quilt on your home machine.

To keep your quilt layers together, you can use any of the following methods.

Pin Basting

The pin-basting method uses large quilting pins, or safety pins, to pin through all three layers of the quilt sandwich to keep the fabric smooth and in place for quilting. Start working out from the center, placing the pins about 3–6" (8–15cm) apart all over the quilt. Avoid placing your pins in the seams. The seams can be very bulky and hard to pin, so instead pin around the seams. For a twin-sized quilt, you should use around 100 to 150 basting pins.

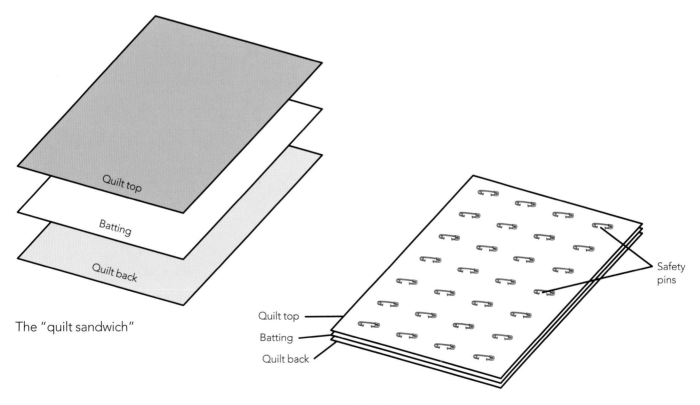

The "quilt sandwich"

Pin basting

Fusible Batting Basting

Another method to baste a quilt is to use fusible batting. This type of batting has an iron-on webbing on both sides to hold your quilt top and quilt back in place. This method can be a little more costly but can also be a time-saver.

Spray Basting

Spray basting is our preferred method of basting because it is economical and fast. To spray baste your quilt, lay your quilt back (right-side down) and tape it to the floor (smooth and taut but not stretched). Lay the batting on top of your quilt back, smoothing out any wrinkles in the batting as well. Then, roll one side of the batting to the middle of the quilt back in a large roll. Start in the middle of the quilt back and apply the basting spray, rolling the batting away from the center and pressing it to the quilt back as you go. Continue spraying small sections of the quilt until you reach the edge. Then roll the second half of the batting and continue just as you did the first side.

The quilt top is basted in the same way as the quilt back. Lay the quilt top right-side up on the batting and spread it out so there are no wrinkles. Roll one side of your quilt top to the middle, then spray small sections of spray basting on the batting, pressing the quilt top onto the batting as you go. Continue spraying in small sections, then pressing and smoothing the quilt top until the first half of the quilt top is basted down. Roll the second side and repeat for the entire quilt top.

Hand Basting

Hand basting a quilt uses long hand stitches to hold the three layers of the quilt in place before machine quilting. Starting in the center and working out, use long, loose stitches to make vertical or horizontal lines every 5–6" (13–15cm). Remove these stitches when you are machine quilting with small scissors or a seam ripper.

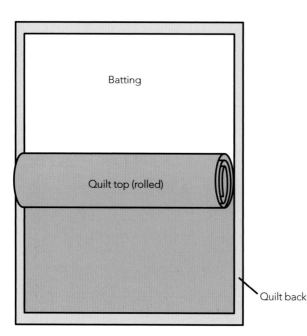

Batting

Quilt top (rolled)

Quilt back

Spray basting

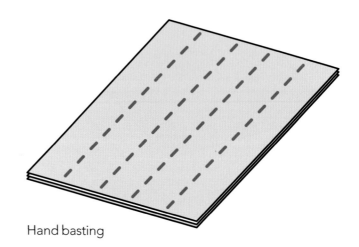

Hand basting

How to Quilt

The actual word *quilting* refers to the process of using a needle and thread to sew and hold the three layers of a quilt in place. There are three methods for doing this:

Machine Quilting

Machine quilting can be done on your home sewing machine using a free-motion quilting foot or a walking foot. In this book there is one quilt and several projects that are quilted on a home sewing machine using a walking foot (the *Log Cabin Quilt* and other projects). For these projects we use straight-line quilting which is described below. Baste your quilt using your preferred method and then use a walking foot on your sewing machine to do the quilting.

1 Use a fabric marker or fabric chalk and a quilting mat and ruler to mark straight lines on the basted quilt.

2 Lengthen your stitch length to 3 or 3.5 and start at the center line of the quilt. Starting at the top of the quilt, stitch all the way down the line, from one end of the quilt to the other.

3 Working from the center of the quilt out, continue stitching down each of the lines you drew.

4 Repeat on the other side until the whole quilt is quilted.

Hand Quilting

Hand quilting is the process of stitching through the three layers of the quilt by hand. The quilt is basted and then quilted using a large hoop or frame and a needle and thread. We won't get into the specifics of hand quilting here, but there are many tutorials online if you'd like to give it a try. It can be a very rewarding experience!

Straight lines drawn on the basted quilt top

TIP

If you don't have a walking foot, you may avoid "creeping" (even when the quilt is basted) by quilting each line in opposite directions.

Long-Arm Quilting

Most of the quilts in this book were quilted by a long-arm quilter. A long-arm quilter does both the basting and quilting process at once using a frame and a long-arm quilting machine. Long-arm quilters often have a variety of quilted patterns to choose from and can add texture and interest to the finished quilt.

How to Make Quilt Binding

There are a number of ways to bind the edges of your quilts. We focus on "straight-edge" binding in this book. Straight-edge binding creates a pop of color along the edge of your quilt while keeping the whole quilt together. Each project will tell you how much fabric you need to make the binding.

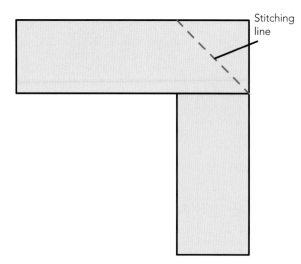

Stitching line

1 Cut 2½" (6.4cm) strips of fabric. Place 2 strips right sides together at a right angle. Mark a diagonal line from the left top corner to the bottom right corner and stitch along this line.

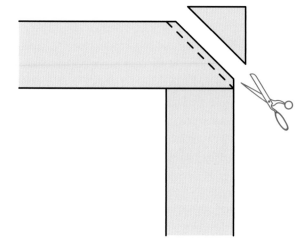

2 Trim off the excess, leaving a ¼" (6mm) seam allowance.

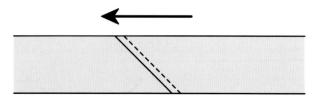

3 Press the binding seam to one side. Continue joining strips until you have a length of binding long enough to surround your quilt plus at least 6" (15.2cm).

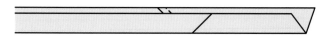

4 Press the binding in half, bringing the long edges together.

How to Attach the Binding

Once you've made a length of binding long enough to wrap around the perimeter of your quilt, you're ready to attach it.

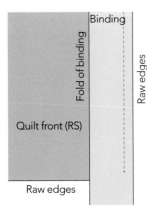

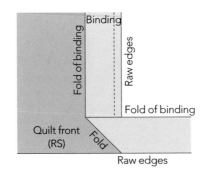

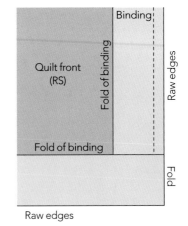

1 Leave a 2½" (6.4cm) tail of binding, and align the raw edges of the binding with the raw edge of your quilt. We suggest beginning your binding in the middle of one side. Stitch the binding in place with a ¼" (6mm) or ⅜" (1cm) seam allowance. Stop and backstitch ¼" (6mm) before you reach the corner of the quilt.

2 Fold the binding at a 90-degree angle away from the quilt top. This is the first step in creating a mitered corner.

3 Fold the binding back, covering the angled fold you created in step 2. Align the raw edge of the binding with the second edge of the quilt top.

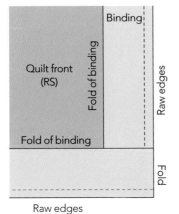

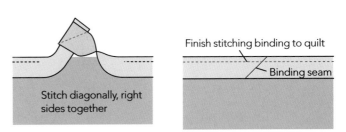

4 Begin stitching again starting on the second edge of your quilt. When you reach the second corner, repeat steps 2 and 3 and continue sewing. Continue working your way around quilt in this manner.

5 When you reach the final edge of the quilt, stop stitching about 2½" (6.4cm) before you reach your starting point. Open the binding on both end pieces and place the right sides together at a right angle. Join the strips with a diagonal seam, as you did in step 1 of How to Make Quilt Binding. Trim the seam allowance to ¼" (6mm), then stitch the binding to the quilt to finish the edge.

Chapter Two
THE NINE PATCH

Quilts often tell a story: a story about the era in which they were made, the conditions under which they were made and the women who created them. Over the years, countless quilt block patterns have been designed, but the humble Nine Patch has remained a constant through all the changes, carrying with it the stories of its creators.

A Nine Patch quilt block is exactly what the name suggests: one quilt block made up of nine square patches. During the westward expansion of the United States, Nine Patch quilt blocks became very popular. Because of their simplistic design, they were relatively fast to put together, and the small patches made it easy for frontier women to use whatever fabric they had on hand to create their blocks. These early quilts tell the tale of the strong women who assembled them using scraps of clothing, ribbon and hand-dyed fabrics.

Today Nine Patch quilts still tell the stories of those who create them. Through size, color and fabric choices, they continue to not only provide warmth, but also a history of the time in which they were created.

How to Make a Nine Patch Quilt Block

To make a Nine Patch block, you'll need nine squares cut to the exact same size. (In this chapter's featured quilt, the squares used in each Nine Patch block measure 2½" [6.4cm].) The finished block measures 6" (15.2cm); with seam allowances, it measures 6½" (16.5cm).

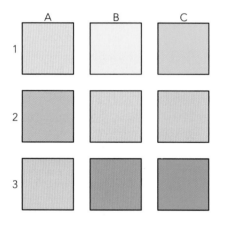

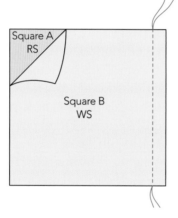

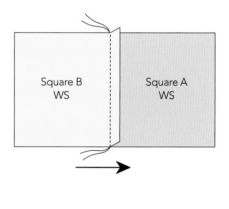

1 Cut your squares to the necessary size. Arrange the squares in your desired layout.

2 Starting in row 1, place squares A and B on top of each other, right sides together. Stitch down one side using a ¼" (6mm) seam allowance.

3 On the wrong side, press the seam toward square A.

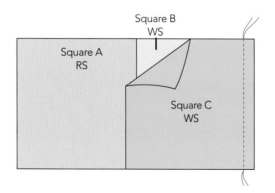

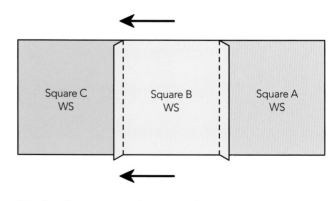

4 Next, place squares C and B from row 1 on top of each other, right sides together. Stitch down one side using a ¼" (6mm) seam allowance.

5 On the wrong side, press the seam toward square C.

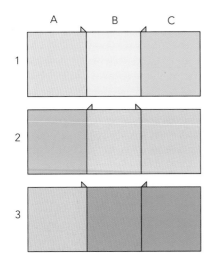

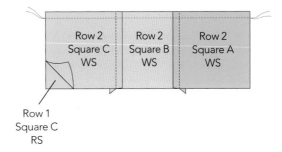

Row 2
Square C
WS

Row 2
Square B
WS

Row 2
Square A
WS

Row 1
Square C
RS

6 Repeat steps 2–5 to complete rows 2 and 3. Note: On row 2, press both the first and second seams toward square B.

Press row 3 in the same manner as row 1. This method of pressing will allow your seams to nestle together nicely and give your blocks a smooth, crisp finish.

7 Place row 2 on top of row 1, right sides together. Align the seams from each row and pin in place. Stitch the rows together using a ¼" (6mm) seam allowance.

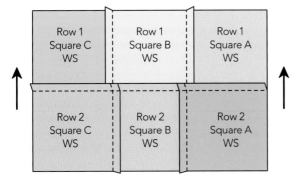

8 On the wrong side, press the seam toward row 1.

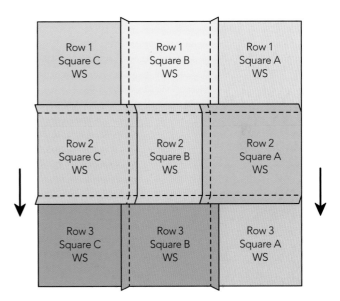

9 Repeat the same process to stitch row 2 to row 3. When pressing, press the seam toward row 3.

10 Turn your block right-side up and give the top a good pressing. Repeat these steps to make as many Nine Patch blocks as you need for your project.

NINE PATCH PILLOW

Makes one 18" (45.7cm) pillow

MATERIALS

¼ yard (23cm) floral fabric

1 yard (1m) white fabric

¼ yard (23cm) solid color coordinating fabric

Matching thread

Batting

Basting spray

Removable fabric marker

Quilting ruler

1 ball of gray yarn (for tassels)

4" (10.2cm) piece of cardstock

18" (45.7cm) pillow form

Walking foot (for sewing machine)

CUTTING INSTRUCTIONS

Floral Fabric
Cut (4) 6½" (16.5cm) squares

White Fabric
Cut (4) 6½" (16.5cm) squares
Cut (2) 18½" × 12" (47cm × 30.5cm) pieces for the back

Solid Fabric
Cut (1) 6½" (16.5cm) square

Batting
Cut (1) 22" (55.9cm) square

"Any time women come together with a collective intention, it's a powerful thing. Whether it's sitting down making a quilt, in a kitchen preparing a meal, in a club reading the same book, or around the table playing cards or planning a birthday party, when women come together with a collective intention, magic happens."

—Phylicia Rashad

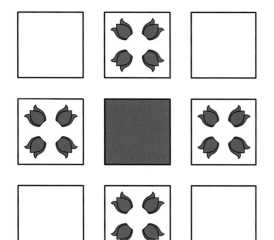

Figure 1

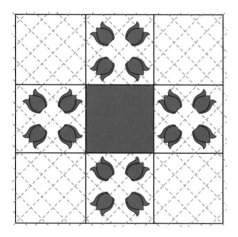

Figure 2

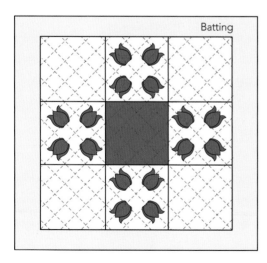

Figure 3

1 Lay out your Nine Patch in the pattern shown in **Figure 1**.

2 Assemble your Nine Patch (which will be the front of your pillow), following the instructions in How to Make a Nine Patch Quilt Block at the beginning of this chapter.

3 Use a fabric marker and quilting ruler to mark lines ½" (1.3cm) apart diagonally across the pillow on the bias to create a crosshatch pattern (**Figure 2**).

4 Use the basting spray to baste the batting to the wrong side of the pillow top (**Figure 3**).

5 Attach the walking foot to your sewing machine and quilt down the marked lines. Quilt each row in the opposite direction than the previous row.

6 Trim the batting to the same size as the quilted top.

7 Make 4 tassels. Cut the cardstock into a 4" (10.2cm) square and wrap the yarn around the cardstock square 20 times. Slip a short length of yarn through one end of the tassel. Do not cut this yarn, you will use it to attach the tassel to the pillow.

Cut through the other end of the yarn and slide the yarn off the cardstock (**Figure 4**). Tie your tassel together 1½" (3.8cm) from the uncut end of your tassel, making sure the length of yarn for attaching the tassel is enclosed in the loop (**Figure 5**).

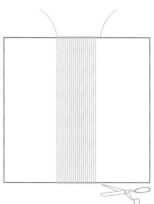

Figure 4

Figure 5

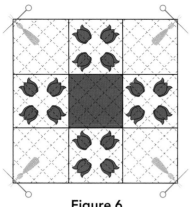

Figure 6

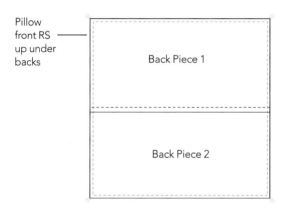

Pillow front RS up under backs

Back Piece 1

Back Piece 2

Figure 8

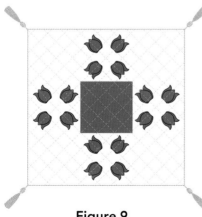

Figure 9

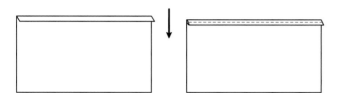

Figure 7

8 Pin the tassels to the 4 corners of the pillow front, facing in (**Figure 6**).

9 On the first backing piece, fold 1 long edge down ½" (1.3cm) toward the wrong side of the fabric and press. Fold the same edge down another ½" (1.3cm) toward the wrong side and press again. Stitch the edge in place using a scant ½" (1.3cm) seam allowance. Repeat on the second backing piece (**Figure 7**).

10 Lay the pillow top right-side up on your work surface. The tassels should be on top of the pillow with the 2 tassel strings extending past the perimeter of the pillow. You will catch these strings in your seam.

Lay the backing pieces right-sides down on top of the pillow front. The hemmed edges will overlap to create an envelope pouch.

11 Pin the pillow front and backs in place. Stitch around the entire perimeter of the pillow using a ¼" (6mm) seam allowance (**Figure 8**).

12 Turn the pillow cover right-sides out. Press the pillow, then stuff with the pillow form (**Figure 9**).

TIP

PRACTICE, PRACTICE, PRACTICE!

There is no book, website or tutorial that can teach as much or as well as old-fashioned, hands-on practice. As you work through the different blocks in this book, don't be afraid to practice making the blocks a few times before making the "final" blocks for your project. The more you practice, the better your quilting will become! As you continue on your quilting journey, you will discover tips, tricks and techniques that work for you and your work will become increasingly more precise and professional.

NINE PATCH FABRIC BASKET

Makes one 15" (38.1cm) square basket

MATERIALS

⅓ yard (0.3m) each of 9 coordinating nine-patch fabrics

1¾ yards (1.6m) coordinating fabric (for lining)

⅓ yard (0.3m) fabric (for binding)

Matching thread

Batting

Basting spray

Fusible interfacing

Quilting clips, such as Wonder Clips or binder clips

Removable fabric marker

Quilting ruler

Walking foot (for sewing machine)

CUTTING INSTRUCTIONS

Nine-Patch Fabrics
From each ⅓ yard (0.3m) of coordinating fabrics, cut (5) 6½" (16.5cm) squares. You should have 45 squares total

Lining Fabric
Cut (5) 17½" (44.5cm) squares

Fusible Interfacing
Cut (5) 18" (45.7cm) squares

Batting
Cut (5) 18" (45.7cm) squares

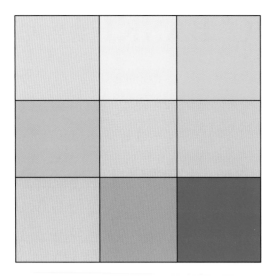

Figure 1

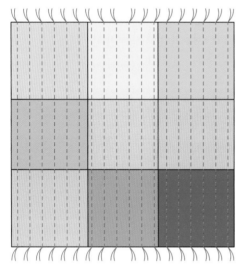

Figure 2

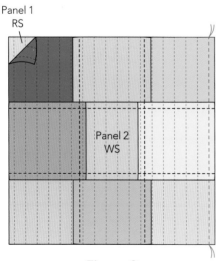

Figure 3

1 Assemble 5 Nine Patch blocks following the instructions in How to Make a Nine Patch Quilt Block at the beginning of this chapter. Each block is a panel of the bag (**Figure 1**).

2 Use a fabric marker and quilting ruler to mark verical lines 1" (2.5cm) apart along each panel.

3 Iron the interfacing to the wrong side of each Nine Patch block, following the manufacturer's instructions.

4 Spray baste the batting squares to the interfacing on each Nine Patch block.

5 Attach the walking foot to your sewing machine and quilt down the marked lines on each panel (**Figure 2**).

6 Lay 2 panels right sides together on your work surface and clip 1 side seam together (the materials are too thick to use pins). With the walking foot still on the sewing machine, sew 1 side seam using a ¼" (6mm) seam allowance (**Figure 3**).

7 Repeat step 6 with 2 of the remaining panels.

8 Clip the joined panels made in steps 6 and 7, right sides together, to form a square. Stitch the seams using a ½" (1.3cm) seam allowance (**Figure 4**).

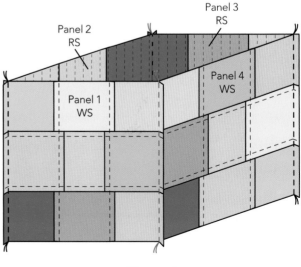

Figure 4

9 Clip the bottom panel, right sides together, to the bottom of the square made in the previous step. Stitch around the edges of the bottom using a ½" (1.3cm) seam allowance (**Figure 5**). Turn the basket right-side out.

10 Following the method used in steps 6–9, join 4 of the lining pieces into a square using a ¼" (6mm) seam allowance. Sew the bottom square in place using a ¼" (6mm) seam allowance.

Note: This is the trickiest part of making the basket. Sew slowly and carefully, remembering to pivot at each corner.

11 Turn the lining wrong-side out and slide it into the fabric basket (**Figure 6**).

12 With the fabric lining inside the basket, baste stitch around the top of the basket to secure the outside panels to the lining (**Figure 7**).

13 Make 2½ yards (2.3m) of binding for the top of the basket following the instructions in Chapter 1.

14 Turn the basket wrong-side out and stitch the raw edges of the binding to the top inside edge of the basket (**Figure 8**). Turn the basket right-side out, then turn the binding to the outside of the basket and stitch in place (**Figure 9**).

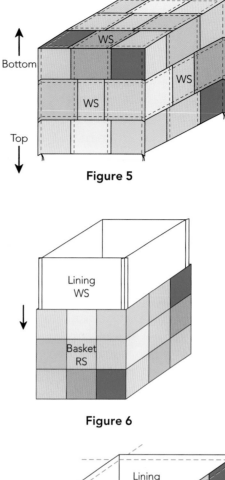

Figure 5

Figure 6

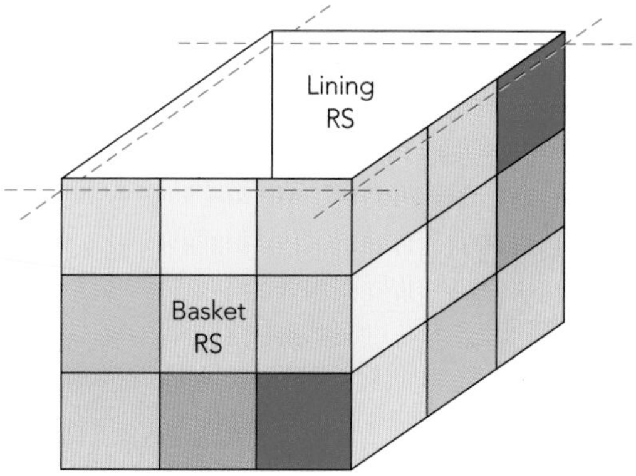

Figure 7

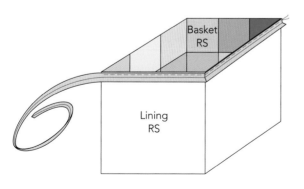

Figure 8

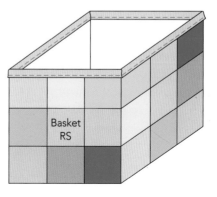

Figure 9

NINE PATCH QUILT

Finished Dimensions: 59" × 59" (150cm × 150cm)

MATERIALS

⅓ yard (0.3m) each of 12 coordinating Nine Patch fabrics (A–L)

1 yard (0.9m) cream fabric (M)

½ yard (0.5m) border fabric

3 yards (2.7m) backing fabric

½ yard (0.5m) binding fabric

Matching thread

65" × 65" (165.1cm × 165.1cm) of batting

CUTTING INSTRUCTIONS

6½" (16.5cm) Squares

Fabric A: cut 4

Fabric B: cut 5

Fabric C: cut 3

Fabric D: cut 3

Fabric E: cut 5

Fabric F: cut 3

Fabric G: cut 4

Fabric H: cut 3

Fabric I: cut 3

Fabric J: cut 3

Fabric K: cut 2

Fabric L: cut 2

2½" (6.4cm) Squares

Fabric A: cut 16

Fabric B: cut 20

Fabric C: cut 13

Fabric D: cut 9

Fabric E: cut 17

Fabric F: cut 12

Fabric G: cut 16

Fabric H: cut 14

Fabric I: cut 12

Fabric J: cut 10

Fabric K: cut 10

Fabric L: cut 11

Fabric M: cut 200 (yes, 200!)

Border Fabric

Cut (2) 3" × 47½" (7.6cm × 120.7cm) strips

Cut (2) 3" × 53½" (7.6cm × 135.9cm) strips

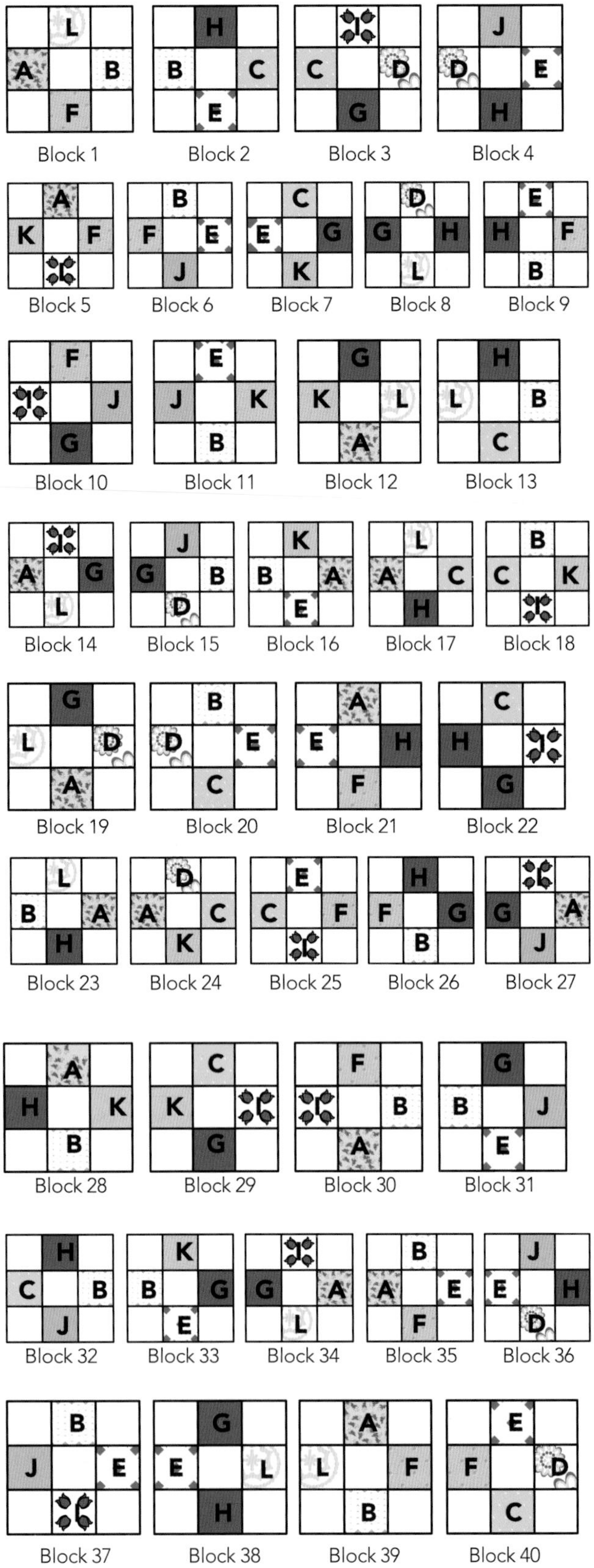

Block 1 Block 2 Block 3 Block 4

Block 5 Block 6 Block 7 Block 8 Block 9

Block 10 Block 11 Block 12 Block 13

Block 14 Block 15 Block 16 Block 17 Block 18

Block 19 Block 20 Block 21 Block 22

Block 23 Block 24 Block 25 Block 26 Block 27

Block 28 Block 29 Block 30 Block 31

Block 32 Block 33 Block 34 Block 35 Block 36

Block 37 Block 38 Block 39 Block 40

Figure 1

1 Following the instructions at the beginning of this chapter for Nine Patch blocks, assemble all of the Nine Patch blocks. **Figure 1** shows the layout for each block row by row. Square up each block as shown in Chapter 1 to 6½" (16.5cm).

2 Using the Quilt Diagram as a guide, lay out the blocks in row 1. Place the second block on top of the first, right sides together. Sew down the right side with a ¼" (6mm) seam allowance (**Figure 2**).

3 Open these blocks and lay them right sides down. Press the seam from the back toward the solid square (**Figure 3**).

4 Take the third square in row 1. Place it on top of the second square, right sides together, and sew down the side with a ¼" (6mm) seam allowance.

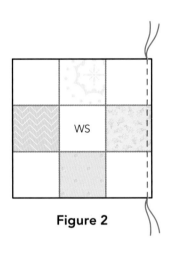

Figure 2

Figure 3

5 Open the piece and lay it right-side down. Press the seam from the back toward the solid square. Pressing the block in this manner will allow you to nest your seams and give the quilt a professional finish. For more information on nesting your seams, see Chapter 1.

6 Continue sewing the blocks across row 1 and pressing the seams toward the solid squares until row 1 is complete.

7 Repeat the process outlined in steps 2–6 to assemble row 2.

8 Place row 2 on top of row 1, right sides together. Align the seams of the rows and pin in place. Sew the rows together down the right side using a ¼" (6mm) seam allowance (**Figure 4**). Press the seam in either direction.

9 Lay out and assemble rows 3 and 4, rows 5 and 6, and rows 7 and 8 following the same method as rows 1 and 2. Lay out and assemble row 9, but do not sew it to another row.

10 Place the rows 3 and 4 unit on top of the rows 1 and 2 unit, right sides together. Pin the units together and sew down the right side with a ¼" (6mm) seam allowance. Press. Continue adding rows until all the rows have been joined, including row 9 at the end. Press all the seams in the same direction.

11 Pin a 3" × 47½" (7.6cm × 120.7cm) border strip across the top of the quilt, right sides together. Sew the border strip in place using a ¼" (6mm) seam allowance (**Figure 5**).

Repeat step 11 to join a border strip to the bottom of the quilt.

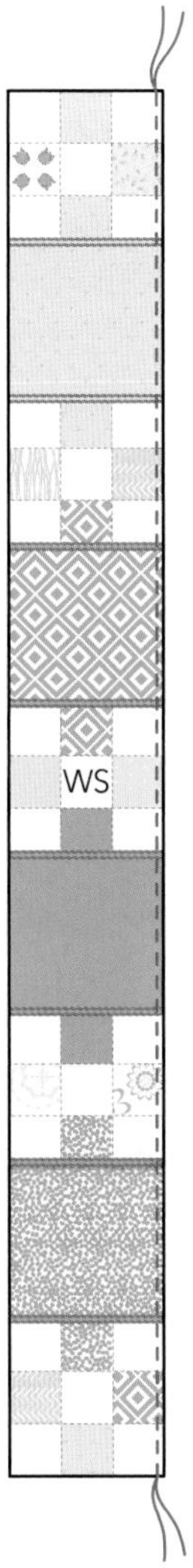

Figure 4

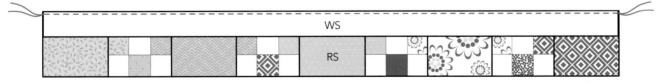

Figure 5

12 Pin one of the 3" × 53½" (7.6cm × 135.9cm) border strips to a side of the quilt, right sides together. Sew the strip in place using a ¼" (6mm) seam allowance. Repeat on the other side of the quilt.

13 Assemble a backing of your choice that measures 60" (152.4cm) square. (For backing instructions, see Chapter 1.)

14 Baste and quilt your quilt according to the directions in Chapter 1 or take your quilt to a long-arm quilter.

15 Make your binding and bind your quilt using the instructions in Chapter 1.

TIP

LABEL YOUR ROWS

Because this quilt is constructed using many blocks and rows, it may be helpful to mark each row, identifying the lead block for each numbered row. With all these blocks, it's easy to sew them together in the wrong order. Trust us...we've all done it!

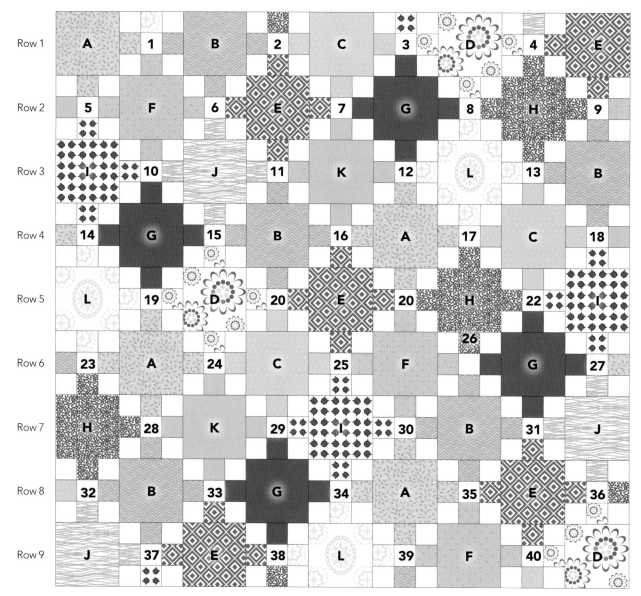

Quilt Diagram

Chapter Three
THE HALF-SQUARE TRIANGLE

The Half-Square Triangle may be one of the most versatile and commonly used of all quilt blocks. Often called "HSTs" or "triangle squares," these blocks can be used in countless ways to assemble a wide variety of quilt designs, from simple geometric layouts to complex patterns.

While the simplistic design of the Half-Square Triangle can stand alone, it is generally used as a building block to create a plethora of other well-known quilt blocks, such as the Pinwheel, the Starflower, Broken Dishes, the Churn Dash and the Bear Paw. But its usefulness doesn't end with building other blocks. Half-Square Triangles are also used to construct popular patterns like chevron, houndstooth and zigzag designs. If you look closely at almost any patchwork quilt you will likely spot more than one Half-Square Triangle block.

Learning to accurately create this one simple block will allow you to make an infinite variety of quilts.

How to Make a Half-Square Triangle Block

To make a Half-Square Triangle quilt block you will need two squares of fabric that are the exact same size but are cut from different prints. In this section we will be using one white square and one colored square that both measure 6" (15.2cm). The finished block is 5" (12.7cm). You'll square it to 5½" (14cm), which includes the seam allowance.

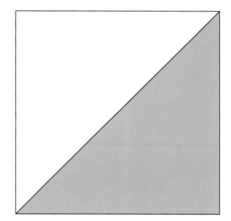

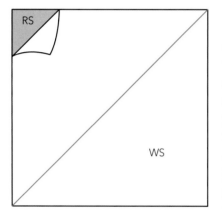

1 Place the white square on top of the colored square, right sides together. Use a fabric marker to draw a diagonal line from corner to corner across the wrong side of the white fabric square.

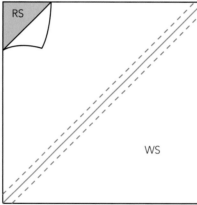

2 Stitch along both sides of the diagonal line, leaving ¼" (6mm) between the diagonal line and your stitching.

3 Cut along the diagonal line, separating your square into 2 pieces.

4 Open the 2 new squares and place them right-side down. Press the seams away from the white, toward the darker colored fabric.

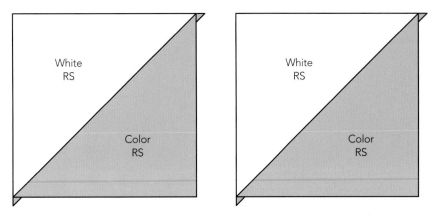

5 Square blocks to an even 5½" × 5½" (14cm × 14cm). (For squaring instructions, see Chapter 1.) Repeat to make as many blocks as needed for your project.

ON MAKING THINGS BY HAND

For many years as I was growing up, I watched my mom spend the pre-holiday season sewing scores of clothes to dress boxes full of dolls. These dolls would then be paired with an outfit and given to children at a local hospital for Christmas. At the time my mom wasn't a huge fan of sewing. And yet, there she was making all these miniature outfits to be given away to children and families she had never met. Reflecting on this now, I think this was my first real lesson in understanding that sewing (and quilting) is usually done for someone other than the person doing the work. All those hours spent with the needle and cloth—the care ,the thought, the love—all of it is meant to be given away. Which I now realize is part of the reason that handmade items carry with them such power and are so precious.

— liZ

HALF-SQUARE TRIANGLE DOLL QUILT

Finished Dimensions: 20" × 20" (50.8cm × 50.8cm)

MATERIALS

¼ yard (23cm) each of 4 different fabrics

½ yard (0.5m) white fabric

23" (58.4cm) square of cotton batting

¾ yard (0.7m) of backing fabric

Basting spray

Removable fabric marker

Quilting ruler

Walking foot (for sewing machine)

CUTTING INSTRUCTIONS

Fabric A
Cut (2) 6" (15.2cm) squares

Fabric B
Cut (2) 6" (15.2cm) squares

Fabric C
Cut (2) 6" (15.2cm) squares

Fabric D
Cut (2) 6" (15.2cm) squares

White Fabric
Cut (8) 6" (15.2cm) squares

Backing Fabric
Cut (1) 23" (58.4cm) square

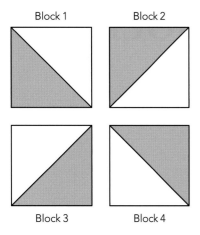

Block 1   Block 2

Block 3   Block 4

Figure 1

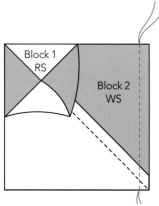

Block 1
RS

Block 2
WS

Figure 2

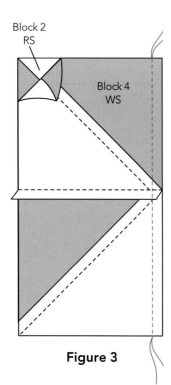

Block 2
RS

Block 4
WS

Figure 3

1 Pair each of the colored squares with a white square and follow the directions at the beginning of the chapter to make Half-Square Triangle blocks. Square them up to 5½" (14cm) square. You'll have 4 blocks for each color combination, 16 blocks total.

2 Lay 4 blocks of the same color in a pinwheel pattern (**Figure 1**).

3 Lay block 2 on top of block 1, right sides together. Stitch down the right side of the blocks with a ¼" (6mm) seam allowance (**Figure 2**).

4 Open the blocks and lay them right-side down. Press the seam toward the darker fabric.

5 Lay block 4 on top of block 3, right sides together. Stitch down the right side of the blocks with a ¼" (6mm) seam allowance.

6 Open the blocks and lay them right-side down. Press the seam toward the darker fabric.

7 Place the blocks 3 and 4 unit on top of the blocks 1 and 2 unit, right sides together. Block 4 should be on top of block 2, block 3 on top of block 1. Stitch down the right side of the blocks with a ¼" (6mm) seam allowance (**Figure 3**).

8 Open the blocks and lay them right side down. Press the seam to the right. You have made 1 pinwheel block. Repeat steps 2 through 8 to make the remaining 3 pinwheel blocks.

9 Place 2 of the pinwheel blocks right sides together and stitch down the right side with a ¼" (6mm) seam allowance (**Figure 4**).

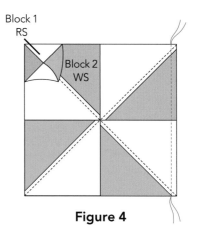

Block 1
RS

Block 2
WS

Figure 4

10 Open the blocks and lay them right-side down. Press the seam to the right.

11 Repeat steps 9 and 10 with the remaining 2 pinwheel blocks, but this time, press the seam to the left. This will help the seams nestle smoothly when the 2 units are joined (**Figure 5**).

12 Place the second pinwheel unit on top of the first, right sides together. Pin the units together, and sew down a long edge with a ¼" (6mm) seam allowance (**Figure 6**). Press the seam in either direction. Press the quilt top on the right side.

13 Use a fabric marker to draw lines on your quilt top ½" (1.3cm) apart on the bias (**Figure 7**).

14 Baste your quilt following the directions in Chapter 1.

15 Attach a walking foot to your sewing machine and quilt down the drawn lines.

16 Trim and bind your quilt following the directions in Chapter 1.

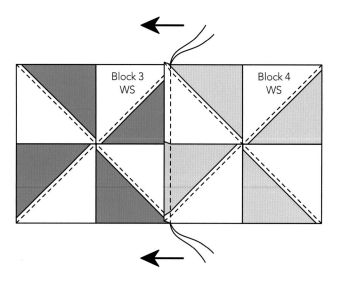

Figure 5

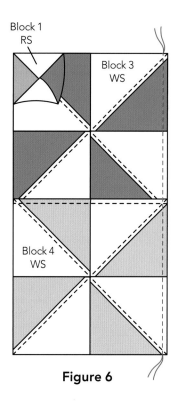

Figure 6

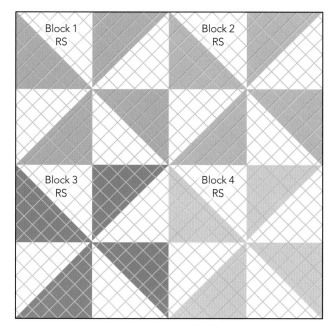

Figure 7

HALF-SQUARE TRIANGLE DREAM BANNER

Makes one 108" (274.3cm) banner

MATERIALS

⅛ yard (11cm) each of 5 colored fabrics

½ yard (0.5m) white fabric

⅛ yard (11cm) cream felt

3 yards (2.7m) pom-pom trim

Iron-on 4" (10.2cm) letters (to spell DREAM)

Coordinating thread

Walking foot (for sewing machine; optional)

Pinking shears

CUTTING INSTRUCTIONS

White Fabric
Cut (10) 4½" (11.4cm) squares

Colored Fabrics
Cut (2) 4½" (11.4cm) squares from each colored fabric (10 squares total)

Cream Felt
Cut (5) 8" (20.3cm) squares

WHY I QUILT

I am often asked the question, "Why do you quilt?" or "Why do you sew?" and there are so many answers, it's hard to choose just one. But there is always one thing that sticks out in my mind: Sewing is something I do everyday that cannot be undone. That's why I started sewing again. I was a new mom who had left a teaching career I loved and I found myself in the depths of laundry and dishes. As much as I loved being a mom, I also yearned for just one thing that would stay constant and not get dirty. Sewing became that one thing for me. I could sew for ten minutes or so every day and it would stay. It gave me a sense of accomplishment even on those days that I hadn't accomplished anything else.

— Elizabeth

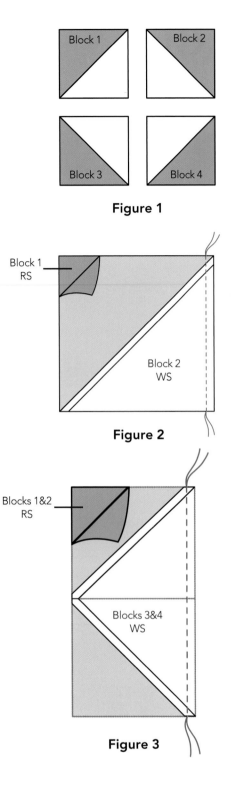

Figure 1

Figure 2

Figure 3

1 Match the white and colored squares to make 20 Half-Square Triangles following the directions at the beginning of the chapter. Square up the blocks to 4" (10.2cm) square.

2 Lay out 4 blocks of the same color with the white centers facing in (**Figure 1**).

3 Place block 2 on top of block 1, right sides together. Stitch down the white side with a ¼" (6mm) seam allowance (**Figure 2**). Press the seam to the right on the wrong side.

4 Place block 4 on top of block 3, right sides together. Stitch down the white side with a ¼" (6mm) seam allowance. Press the seam to the left on the wrong side.

5 Place the 2 units you just created right sides together. The white edge on each should align. Pin the units in place, carefully aligning the seams. Sew down the white edge with a ¼" (6mm) seam allowance (**Figure 3**).

6 Repeat steps 2–5 to create 4 more blocks.

7 Press and square each of the blocks to 7½" (19.1cm) following the instructions in Chapter 1 (**Figure 4**).

8 Place each completed quilt block right side up onto a felt square. Pin in place and sew around the perimeter of the quilt block with a ¼" (6mm) seam allowance.

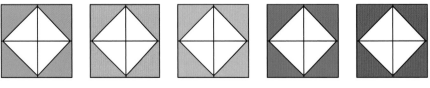

Figure 4

9 Quilt each block as desired. In the banner shown, we used the stitch-in-the-ditch method (walking foot optional).

10 Use pinking shears to cut around each block, leaving a scant ¼" (6mm) border around the block (**Figure 5**).

11 Following the manufacturer's directions, press an iron-on letter onto the white center of each block (**Figure 6**).

12 Lay out your blocks, evenly spacing them. Lay the pom-pom trim along the tops of the blocks, centering the trim so the lengths on either end of your blocks are even. Pin the trim in place.

13 Stitch the pom-pom trim in place (**Figure 7**).

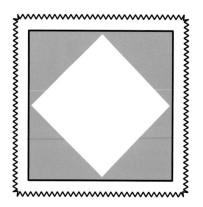

Figure 5

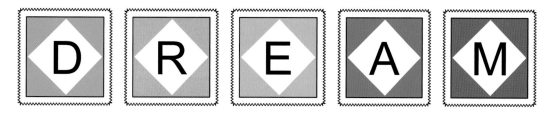

Figure 6

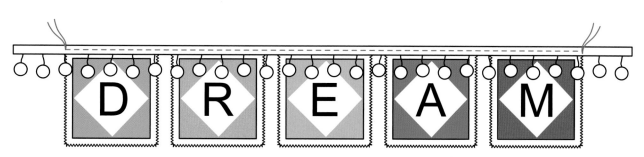

Figure 7

HALF-SQUARE TRIANGLE QUILT

Finished Dimensions: 72" × 72" (182.9cm × 182.9cm)

MATERIALS

2¼ yards (2.1m) white fabric

1 yard (0.9m) pink fabric (can be 1 fabric or several pink fabrics)

1 yard (0.9m) green fabric (can be 1 fabric or several green fabrics)

⅔ yard (0.6m) orange fabric (can be 1 fabric or several orange fabrics)

½ yard (0.5m) cream fabric (can be 1 fabric or several cream fabrics)

4½ yards (4.1m) backing fabric

⅔ yard (0.6cm) binding fabric

Matching thread

78" (198.1cm) square of batting (queen size)

CUTTING INSTRUCTIONS

6" (15.2cm) Squares

White fabric: cut 115

Pink fabric: cut 50

Green fabric: cut 34

Orange fabric: cut 20

Cream fabric: cut 11

5" (12.7cm) Squares

White fabric: cut 64

FRIDAY NIGHT QUILTS

For both of our families, Friday nights and quilts have become synonymous. After eating pizza, we take turns picking a movie to watch together as a family. Quilts are an important part of the night—each of the kiddos is wrapped snuggly in their favorite handmade quilt. At the end of the night, as we look at our families surrounded by the love of each handmade quilt, we feel incredibly grateful that we have this time together and hope the tradition will be passed on through our quilts.

— Elizabeth & liZ

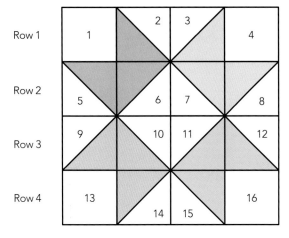

Figure 1

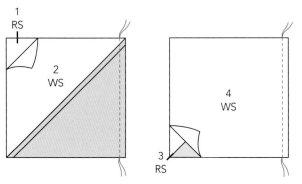

Figure 2

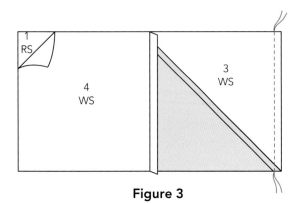

Figure 3

1 Match each of the white 6" (15.2cm) squares with a colored square and follow the directions at the beginning of the chapter for making Half-Square Triangles. Be sure to press and square your blocks to 5" (12.7cm).

2 Arrange the individual Half-Square Triangle blocks and the white 5" (12.7cm) squares into Ribbon Star blocks (see **Figure 1**). The arrangement of the colors in this quilt is chosen randomly. Use any 4 colors you like in your ribbon star blocks. If you choose to plan ahead, lay out each of the Ribbon Star blocks before you start sewing to make sure you're happy with the color combinations within each block.

3 Starting in row 1 of the Ribbon Star block, sew your blocks together. Place block 2 on top of block 1, right sides together. Sew down the right side with a ¼" (6mm) seam. Repeat with blocks 3 and 4 in row 1 (**Figure 2**).

4 Open the units and press the seams on the wrong side (**Figure 3**).

5 Lay the block 3 and 4 unit on top of the block 1 and 2 unit, wrong sides together. Block 4 should be on top of block 1. Pin in place and stitch down the right side with a ¼" (6mm) seam allowance.

6 Open this new unit and press the seam on the wrong side.

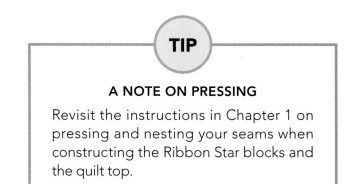

TIP

A NOTE ON PRESSING

Revisit the instructions in Chapter 1 on pressing and nesting your seams when constructing the Ribbon Star blocks and the quilt top.

7 Repeat steps 3–6 to complete the remaining 3 rows of the Ribbon Star block.

8 Pin row 1 and row 2 of the Ribbon Star block wrong sides together, aligning the seams. Sew the rows together with a ¼" (6mm) seam allowance. Press the seam up.

9 Pin row 3 and row 4 of the Ribbon Star block right sides together, aligning the seams. Sew the rows together with a ¼" (6mm) seam allowance. Press the seam up.

10 Pin the row 1 and 2 unit to the row 3 and 4 unit, right sides together. Align the seams and sew with a ¼" (6mm) seam allowance. Press the seam up.

11 Repeat steps 2–10 to make 16 Ribbon Star blocks. Square up the blocks to 18½" (45.7cm) square.

12 Lay out 4 Ribbon Star blocks for the first row of your quilt (**Figure 4**).

13 Place block 2 on top of block 1, right sides together, and pin in place. Sew down the right side with a ¼" (6mm) seam allowance. Repeat with blocks 3 and 4 (**Figure 5**).

14 Place the block 3 and 4 unit on top of the block 1 and 2 unit, right sides together. Block 4 should be on top of block 1. Pin in place, aligning the seams. Sew down the right side with a ¼" (6mm) seam allowance.

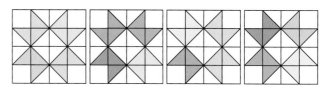

Figure 4

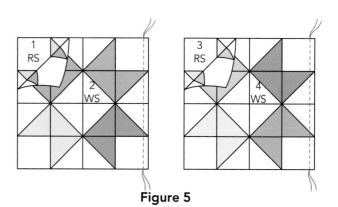

Figure 5

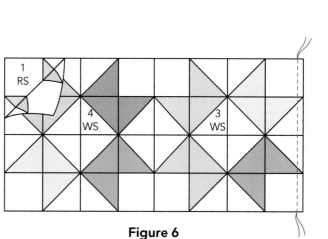

Figure 6

TIP

FIRST QUILT

We recommend that if you're making your first quilt (or even your first couple of quilts), you start with quilts that include basic designs and constructions (like the Half-Square Triangle quilt!) and then continue to work your way through more complicated designs and patterns.

15 Place row 1 right-side down and press the seams.

16 Repeat steps 12–15 to make the remaining 3 rows of your quilt.

17 Pin rows 1 and 2, right sides together, and sew with a ¼" (6mm) seam allowance. Repeat with rows 3 and 4.

18 Place the row 1 and 2 unit on top of the row 3 and 4 unit, right sides together. Pin in place, aligning the seams. Sew the units together with a ¼" (6mm) seam allowance.

19 Open the quilt top and place it right-side down. Press the quilt on the wrong side.

20 Assemble a backing that measures 86" (218.4cm) square. See Chapter 1 for directions.

21 Baste and quilt your quilt as explained in Chapter 1 or send your quilt to a long-arm quilter.

22 Make your binding and bind your quilt following the directions in Chapter 1.

Finished Quilt Top

Chapter Four
THE CHURN DASH

The Churn Dash quilt block has as many as twenty-one different names and variations! Some of these include Broken Plate, Double Monkey Wrench, Hens and Chickens, Hole in the Barn Door, Love Knot and Old Mill Design.

Many quilt blocks were given names according to what the block resembles, and this block is no exception. The Churn Dash resembles the equipment used to churn butter. The churn refers to the container in which the butter is mixed, while the dash refers to the square cross-shaped stick that is used to do the actual mixing.

While this block does resemble a churn dash, its construction is basically a variation of the Nine Patch quilt block we made in Chapter 2! There are nine squares that make up a Churn Dash quilt block. The outer four squares are made from Half-Square Triangles, the center square is solid and the remaining squares are simply two rectangles sewn together to form a square. The block is fairly simple to construct but the result is beautiful.

How to Make a Churn Dash Quilt Block

These instructions will make a 9" (22.9cm) square finished block. This size block is used in the *Churn Dash Apron* project and the *Churn Dash Potholder* project. The actual *Churn Dash Quilt* size is much larger. You'll need two different fabrics to make this block.

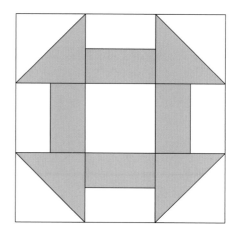

CUTTING INSTRUCTIONS

White Fabric
Cut (2) 4"(10.2cm) squares
Cut (1) 3½" (8.9cm) square
Cut (4) 2" × 3½" (5.1cm × 8.9cm) strips

Colored Fabric
Cut (2) 4"(10.2cm) squares
Cut (4) 2" × 3½" (5.1cm × 8.9cm) strips

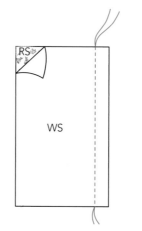

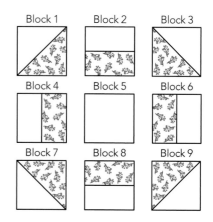

1 Use two 4" (10.2cm) white squares and two 4" (10.2cm) colored squares to make 4 Half-Square Triangle blocks. Refer to the instructions for Half-Square Triangle blocks at the beginning of Chapter 3. Press toward the darker fabric and square up the blocks to 3½" (8.9cm).

2 Place a white rectangle piece on top of a colored rectangle, right sides together. Stitch along a long edge with a ¼" (6mm) seam allowance. Repeat with the remaining rectangles for a total of 4 blocks. Press the seams toward the darker fabric and trim the blocks to 3½" (8.9cm) square.

3 Lay out the blocks in the Churn Dash pattern, using the above illustration as a guide.

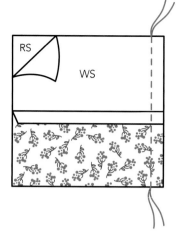

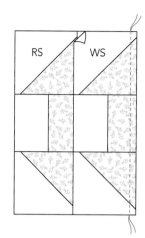

6 Place row 2 on top of row 1, right sides together, and pin in place. Stitch the edge with a ¼" (6mm) seam allowance. Press the seam.

4 Place block 2 on top of block 1, right sides together, and pin in place. Stitch along the right edge with a ¼" (6mm) seam allowance. Press the seam toward block 2.

5 Place block 3 on top of block 2, right sides together, and pin it in place. Stitch along the right edge with a ¼" (6mm) seam allowance. Press the seam toward block 2. Row 1 is complete.

Repeat steps 4 and 5 to complete rows 2 and 3 of the block. Alternate the direction of the pressed seams in each row (see Nesting Your Seams in Chapter 1).

7 Align row 3 on top of row 2, right sides together, and pin in place. Stitch the edge with a ¼" (6mm) seam allowance. Press the seam in either direction.

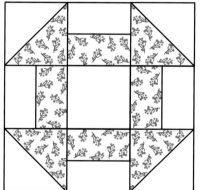

8 Trim the block to a 9½" (24.1cm) square following the directions in Chapter 1.

TIP

CHOOSING FABRICS

Choosing fabrics can be really fun but it can also be tricky! Here are a few tips that we find useful when selecting the fabrics for our projects:

- Solid colored fabrics can help define shapes, especially when paired with patterned prints.
- When using prints, try to include a mixture of small, medium and large scale prints.
- Be thoughtful when mixing prints; it's often best to place small prints next to large prints for optimal contrast. When prints of similar size are placed next to each other, your block design tends to get lost in the similar pattern choices.

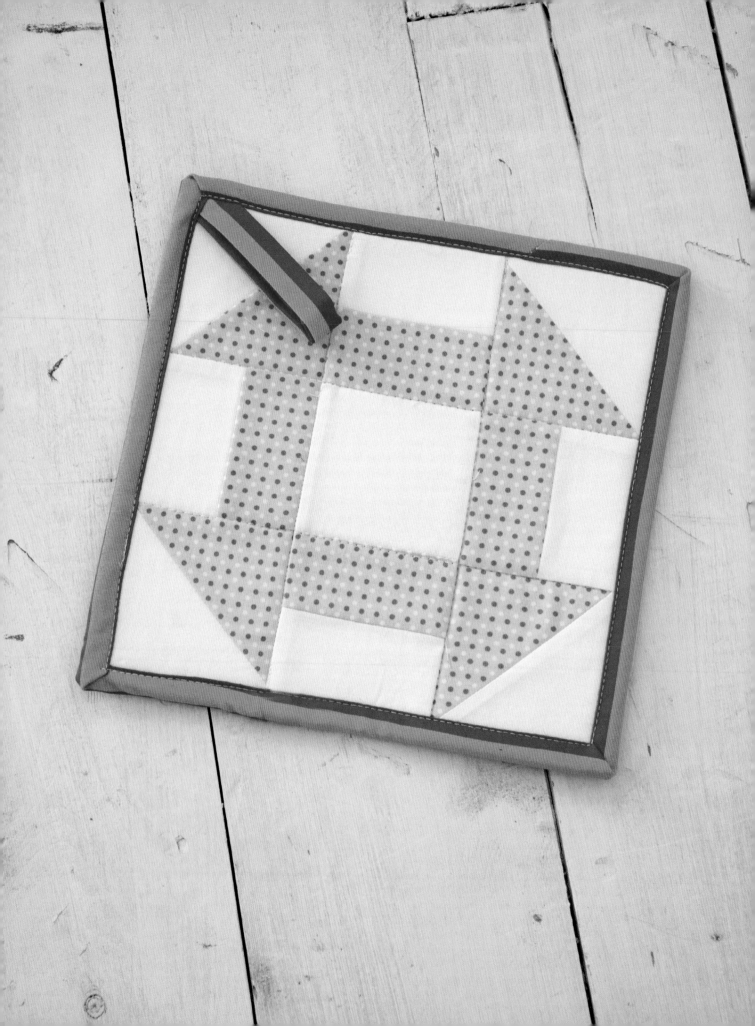

CHURN DASH APRON

Makes one apron

MATERIALS

⅙ yard (15cm) white fabric (for Churn Dash block)

⅓ yard (0.3m) printed fabric (for Churn Dash block)

½ yard (0.5m) solid fabric (for apron body)

½ yard (0.5m) coordinating fabric (for apron ties)

Matching thread

CUTTING INSTRUCTIONS

White Fabric

Cut (2) 4" (10.2cm) squares

Cut (1) 3½" (8.9cm) square

Cut (4) 2" × 3½" (5.1cm × 8.9cm) strips

Printed Fabric

Cut (2) 4" (10.2cm) squares

Cut (4) 2" × 3½" (5.1cm × 8.9cm) strips

Cut (1) 9½" (24.1cm) square (pocket backing)

Apron Body Fabric

Cut (1) 18" × WOF" (45.7cm × WOF) rectangle (see Note)

Apron Tie Fabric

Cut (2) 8" × WOF" (20.3cm × WOF) rectangles

Note: "WOF" stands for "width of fabric."

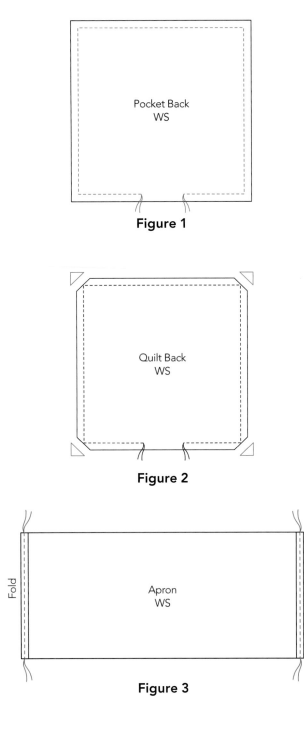

Figure 1

Figure 2

Figure 3

1 Construct a 9½" (24.1cm) Churn Dash block as shown at the beginning of this chapter.

2 Place the quilt block and pocket backing right sides together and pin in place. Stitch around the edge with a ¼" (6mm) seam allowance, leaving a 2" (5.1cm) opening at the bottom of the pocket for turning (**Figure 1**).

3 Trim the 4 corners of the pocket (**Figure 2**), being careful not to clip the seam, then turn the pocket right-side out through the 2" (5.1cm) opening. Use a point turner or pin to get the corners square. Press the pocket, making sure to press the raw edges of the opening toward the inside, matching the seam allowance. Set aside.

4 Fold a ¼" (6mm) seam allowance on the two short edges of the main apron piece to the wrong side. Fold both edges another ¼" (6mm) to the wrong side and press. Stitch the folded edges in place (**Figure 3**).

5 Repeat step 4 on the bottom edge of the apron.

6 Place the pocket right-side up on the front of the main apron piece 4" (10.2cm) from the top and 6" (15.2cm) from the right side. Pin in place, then stitch around the sides and bottom of the pocket, being sure to catch the 2" (5.1cm) opening in the seam (**Figure 4**).

7 Set your sewing machine to a very long basting length and stitch 2 rows of gathering stitches along the top of the main apron piece (**Figure 5**).

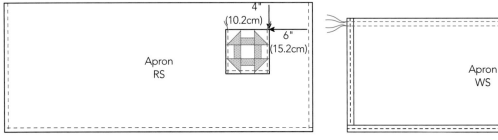

Figure 4

Figure 5

8 Pull the bobbin threads of your gathering stitches and gather the top of the apron body until it measures 25" to 30" (63.5cm to 76.2cm), depending on your preference.

9 Cut 1 of the waistband tie pieces in half (this is to prevent a seam in the middle of your apron's waistband). Align a shorter waistband tie piece with either edge of the long waistband tie piece, right sides together. Pin in place and stitch with a ¼" (6mm) seam allowance. You now have a single strip for the waistband tie (**Figure 6**).

10 Press the short ends of the waistband tie ½" (1.3cm) to the wrong side and stitch in place (**Figure 7**).

11 Fold the waistband tie in half lengthwise, wrong sides together, and press well. Open up and fold the bottom and top raw edges to the middle fold line. Press the top and bottom edges (**Figure 8**). Refold the waistband tie in half.

12 Center the main apron piece along the waistband tie. Sandwich the gathered edge of the apron between the waistband tie layers and pin in place (**Figure 9**).

13 Start at one side of the waistband tie and topstitch around the entire perimeter of the waistband, securing the apron body in place and closing the waistband tie (**Figure 10**).

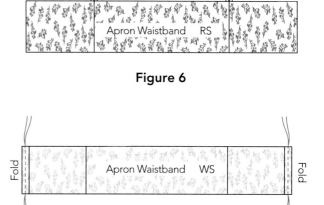

Figure 6

Figure 7

Figure 8

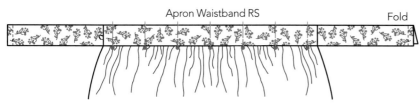

Figure 9

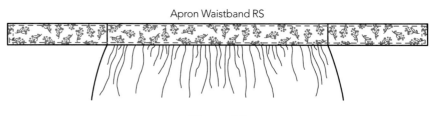

Figure 10

CHURN DASH QUILT

Finished Dimensions: 60" × 60" (152.4cm × 152.4cm)

MATERIALS

2¾ yards (2.5m) print fabric (see Note)

1 yard (0.9m) white fabric

¾ yards (0.7m) binding fabric

3¾ yards (3.4m) backing fabric

Matching thread

Walking foot (for sewing machine; optional)

66" (167.6cm) square of batting

Basting spray (optional)

Note: A non-directional print works best for this quilt.

CUTTING INSTRUCTIONS

Print Fabric

Cut (2) 16" (40.6cm) squares

Cut (1) 15½" (39.4cm) square

Cut (4) 8" × 15½" (20.3cm × 39.4cm) rectangles

Cut (2) 8" × 45½" (20.3cm × 115.6cm) rectangles (short quilt borders)

Cut (2) 8" × 60½" (20.3cm × 153.7cm) rectangles (long quilt borders)

White Fabric

Cut (2) 16" (40.6cm) squares

Cut (4) 8" × 15½" (20.3cm × 39.4cm) rectangles

"Sewing mends the soul."

—Unknown

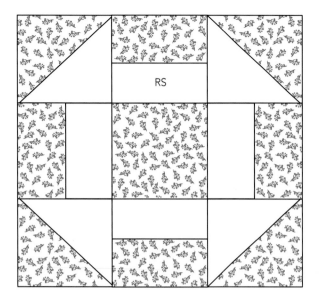

Figure 1

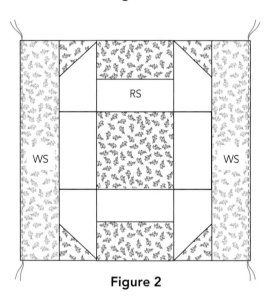

Figure 2

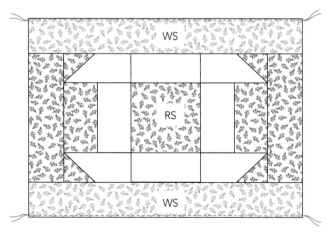

Figure 3

1 The pieces used in the quilt are larger than the pieces in the block instructions at the beginning of the chapter, but the method is the same: Pair a white 16" (40.6cm) square with each print 16" (40.6cm) square. Follow the instructions in Chapter 3 to make 4 Half-Square Triangle blocks and square them up to 15½" (39.4cm).

2 Pair each of the 8" × 15½" (20.3cm × 39.4cm) print rectangles with an 8" × 15½" (20.3cm × 39.4cm) white rectangle. Stitch along the long edge on each pair to make four 15½" (39.4cm) square quilt blocks.

3 Arrange the 4 Half-Square Triangle blocks, the 4 Half-rectangle blocks and the 15½" (39.4) print square into a Churn Dash block, using **Figure 1** as a guide.

Sew the blocks and rows together as instructed at the beginning of the chapter and square up the block to 45½" (115.6cm)

4 Align the long edge of one short quilt border along the side of the quilt and pin in place. Stitch the edge with a ¼" (6mm) seam allowance. Repeat to attach the second short quilt border to the opposite side of the quilt (**Figure 2**). Press the seams.

5 Align the long edge of one long quilt border along the top of the quilt and pin in place. Stitch the edge with a ¼" (6mm) seam allowance. Repeat to attach the second long quilt border to the opposite side of the quilt (**Figure 3**). Press the seams.

6 Prepare a 66" (167.6cm) square quilt backing following the directions in Chapter 1.

7 If you plan to send your quilt to a long-arm quilter, you are finished. If not, follow the basting and quilting instructions in Chapter 1. Square up your quilt to 60" (152.4cm), then make the binding and bind your quilt as explained in Chapter 1.

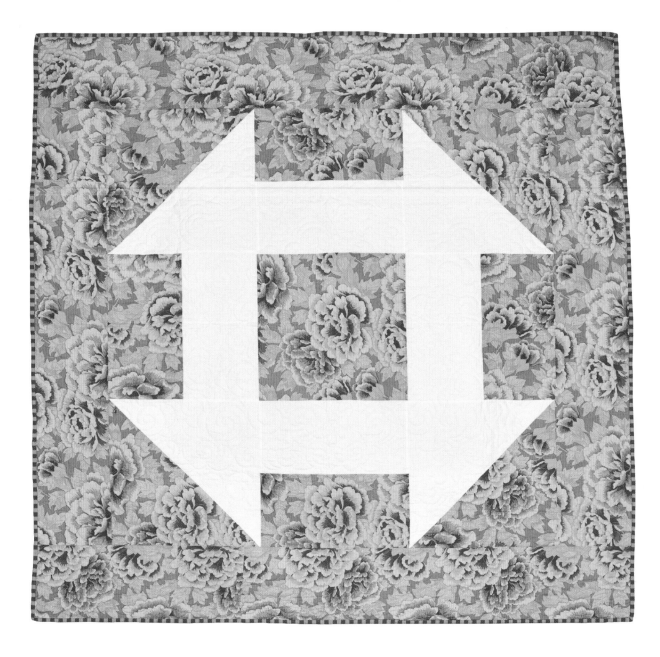

TIP

SQUARING UP YOUR QUILT

To square up your quilt top quickly and easily, fold the quilt horizontally and vertically to see if the edges meet. If they do, your quilt is square. If they don't, you can trim up your quilt top to square it up before you put the binding on.

To more properly square up your quilt top, first find the center of the quilt and measure to each of the sides. If one side is longer, you can trim up each side to make it the same distance from the center of the quilt. Use a quilting ruler and a rotary cutter to trim the sides to be equal distance from the center of the quilt. Repeat for the other two sides as well.

Chapter Five
THE RAIL FENCE

The Rail Fence block is a classic American quilt block whose rise to popularity took place during Colonial times. Family gatherings around the hearth were a common evening practice. So was the tradition of mothers teaching their children to sew simple quilt blocks while they enjoyed the warmth of the fire. It was during these times that many children of that era learned to piece the simple Rail Fence quilt block.

Given its name from the split wooden rail fences of the time, the Rail Fence quilt block quickly became a favorite for quilters. The construction was easy and they were able to use a variety of small fabric scraps.

Over the years the Rail Fence block has enjoyed many different revivals. Early on, it debuted at state fairs sporting only the colors of red, white and blue. Years later, these blocks helped to send information to slaves escaping through the Underground Railroad. This block has been a staple for quilters here on the North American continent and still continues to be a popular block for beginning and advanced quilters alike.

How to Make a Rail Fence Quilt Block

To make a Rail Fence quilt block, cut four different fabrics from selvage edge to selvage edge into 2½" (6.4cm) strips. The finished block measures 8" (20.3cm); square it to 8½" (21.6cm) to account for the seam allowances.

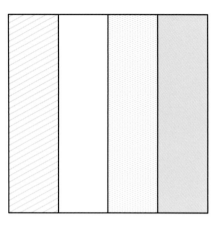

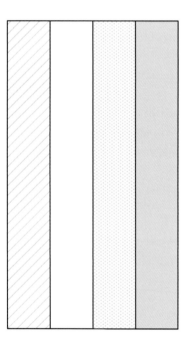

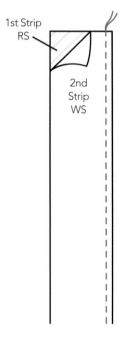

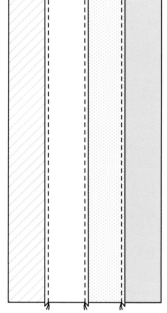

1 Lay out your 4 strips in your desired arrangement.

2 Place the second strip on top of the first, right sides together. Sew down the right edge with a ¼" (6mm) seam allowance.

3 Sew the third and fourth strips together in the same manner, then place the 2 strip sets on top of each other, right sides together. Sew down 1 long edge with a ¼" (6mm) seam.

4 Open the strips and press the seams on the wrong side toward the darker fabrics.

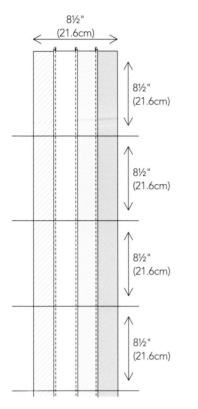

8½"
(21.6cm)

8½"
(21.6cm)

8½"
(21.6cm)

8½"
(21.6cm)

8½"
(21.6cm)

5 You now have an 8½" (21.6cm) wide strip consisting of 4 different fabrics. Cut this strip into 8½" (21.6cm) squares to create the Rail Fence block. You will get approximately 4 to 5 blocks from each strip set, depending on the width of the fabric.

MY FIRST QUILT

Shortly after I had gotten back into sewing, I saw a neighbor walking with her new baby grandson in a stroller. Covering the baby was a bright orange chenille rag quilt. I thought it was one of the most beautiful quilts I had ever seen (it makes me laugh now). The next time I saw that neighbor I got up the courage to ask her how she made her grandson's quilt. She invited me to her house and gave me a short lesson on how to make a chenille rag quilt. She talked in simple terms so I could understand, showed me how to rag and cut the chenille backing and I was sold. I bought flannel that night and sewed up a chenille rag quilt. I think I made about ten or so flannel quilts that first couple of months when I was sewing. I was so proud of those blankets.

I often think about that neighbor and her kindness. I am sure it wasn't a big deal to her to show me how to make that simple baby blanket, but it was my first step into the quilting world, and I am forever grateful.

— Elizabeth

RAIL FENCE PILLOW

Makes one 18" (45.7cm) pillow

MATERIALS

1½ yards (1.4m) white fabric

4 pink fabric scraps each measuring 2½" × 9" (6.4cm × 22.9cm)

2½ yards (2.3m) pink pom-pom trim

Matching thread

Pillow form (see Note)

Zipper foot (for sewing machine)

Note: A 20" (50.8cm) pillow form is larger than the 18½" (47cm) pillow cover and will make a full, fluffy-looking pillow. If you would like a thinner pillow, use an 18" (45.7cm) pillow form.

CUTTING INSTRUCTIONS

White Fabric

Cut (2) 8½" × 5½" (21.6cm × 14cm) pieces

Cut (2) 19" × 5½" (48.3cm × 14cm) pieces

Cut (2) 19" × 12" (48.3cm × 30.5cm) pieces

QUILT GIVING

My neighbor Barb became an unexpected friend to me. I often asked Barb's advice on all sorts of things, and she always gave me the most curt and most sensible advice. A couple of summer's before we moved away, Barb had hip replacement surgery. Before the surgery, she went around the neighborhood telling her neighbors that she didn't want meals brought to her, housekeeping done for her or any other "fusses" made. She was going to be fine on her own and wanted us all to know it.

Unbeknownst to Barb, I began cutting up little squares of fabric to make her a recovery quilt. A few weeks after her surgery, I walked over to her house to give her the handmade gift. I wasn't sure how she'd react, but was determined to give it to her anyway.

I set the quilt in her lap and waited as she stared down at the quilt. When she looked up again, she had tears in her eyes. Barb may not have needed the meals, the housekeeping or any "fusses," but she did appreciate a little extra love from a quilt.

— Elizabeth

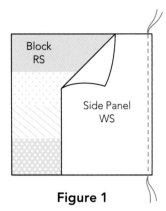

Figure 1

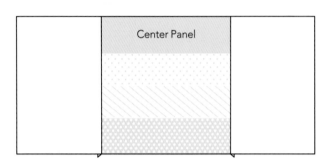

Figure 2

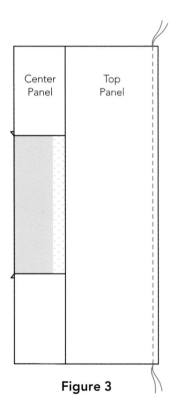

Figure 3

1 Assemble a Rail Fence quilt block from the pink strips, following the instructions at the beginning of the chapter. Square the block to 8½" (21.6cm).

2 Align a long edge of an 8½" × 5½" (21.6cm × 14cm) piece with the Rail Fence block, laying the pieces right sides together. Pin in place, then sew the long edge with a ¼" (6mm) seam allowance (**Figure 1**).

3 Open the pieces and press the seam on the back side away from the Rail Fence block.

4 Repeat steps 2 and 3 to add the other side panel to your Rail Fence block. This completes the center panel of your pillow front (**Figure 2**).

5 Place a 19" × 5½" (48.3cm × 14cm) piece across the top of the center panel, right sides together. Sew the pieces together with a ¼" (6mm) seam allowance (**Figure 3**). Open and press the seam away from the Rail Fence block.

6 Place the remaining 19" × 5½" (48.3cm × 14cm) piece across the bottom of the center panel, right sides together. Sew the pieces together with a ¼" (6mm) seam allowance. Open and press the seam away from the Rail Fence block. The pillow front is now complete (**Figure 4**).

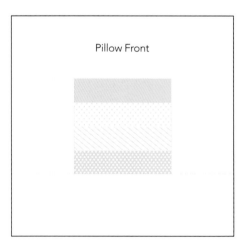

Figure 4

7 Prepare your pillow back: Turn 1 long edge on each 19" × 12" (48.3cm × 30.5cm) piece under ½" (1.3cm) toward the wrong side and press. Turn the folded edges under another ½" (1.3cm) and press again. Stitch the edges using a ½" (1.3cm) seam allowance (**Figure 5**).

8 Set up the zipper foot on your sewing machine and baste the pom-pom trim in place around the perimeter of the pillow front. The pom-poms should face the center of your pillow (**Figure 6**).

9 Layer the pillow backs on top of the pillow front, right sides together. Align the raw edges; the folded edges on the back pieces will overlap. Pin the pieces in place and stitch around the perimeter of the entire pillow with a ¼" (6mm) seam allowance (**Figure 7**).

10 Turn the pillow right-side out and press (**Figure 8**). Fill with your pillow form.

Figure 5

Figure 6

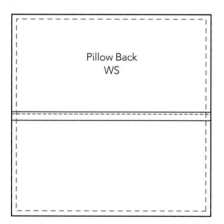

Pillow Back
WS

Figure 7

Figure 8

RAIL FENCE SKIRT

Makes one skirt

MATERIALS

½–2 yards (0.5–1.8m) white fabric (depending on measurements)

Black, white and pink fabric scraps (a total of at least 4 different fabrics) for the Rail Fence blocks

¼ yard (23cm) coordinating fabric for pocket backing

1–2 yards (0.9–1.8m) pink trim for skirt bottom

½–2 yards (0.5–1.8m) of 1" (2.5cm) elastic (based on waist measurement)

Matching thread

Large safety pin

Pinking shears (optional)

CUTTING INSTRUCTIONS

Rail Fence Fabrics
From each of the 4 different fabrics, cut (2) 1½" × 9" (3.8cm × 22.9cm) rectangles (8 rectangles total)

Pocket Backing Fabric
Cut (2) 4½" (11.4cm) squares

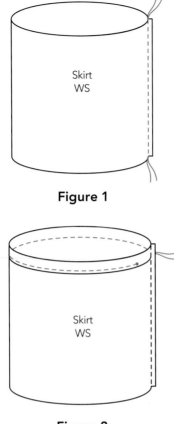

Figure 1

Figure 2

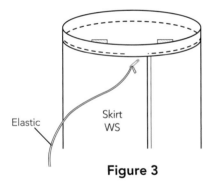

Elastic

Figure 3

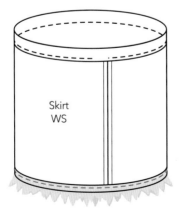

Figure 4

1 Determine the size of the skirt you plan to make: To do this, take the waist measurement of the child for whom you're making the skirt. Double the meaurement and record it. Next, measure the distance from the child's waist to knee. Add 2½" (6.4cm) to this measurement and record it.

2 Cut a rectangle from the white fabric using the measurements from step 1.

3 Fold the rectangle in half, right sides together, matching the short ends of the fabric. Pin along the edge and stitch with a ½" (1.3cm) seam allowance (**Figure 1**). Secure the ends of the seams with backstitching. Press the seam open.

4 Turn the top edge of the skirt down 1½" (3.8cm) toward the wrong side of the fabric. Stitch around the circumference of the skirt, stopping 2" (5.1cm) before you reach your starting point. This opening is where you will thread the elastic. We recommend positioning it near the back seam made in step 3 (**Figure 2**).

5 Cut the elastic 2" (5.1cm) shorter than the waist measurement (before it was doubled). Attach a large safety pin to one end of the elastic. Secure the other end of the elastic by pinning it to the seam allowance. Guide the elastic through the waistband of the skirt (**Figure 3**). Be sure not to twist the elastic. Overlap the ends of the elastic and stitch several times to secure. Tuck the end into the waistband and finish sewing the waistband shut.

6 Turn the hem of the skirt under ½" (1.3cm) toward the wrong side of the fabric, and press. Turn the folded edge under another ½" (1.3) and press. Pin the trim around the wrong side of the hem, then stitch the trim in place, securing the hem close to the inner folded edge at the same time (**Figure 4**).

7 Using the strips cut for the Rail Fence blocks and the instructions at the beginning of the chapter, make 2 Rail Fence blocks measuring 4½" (11.4cm) square (**Figure 5**).

8 Place the pocket backing on top of the pocket front, right sides together. Pin the pieces together, then sew around all edges with a ¼" (6mm) seam allowance. Stop at the bottom, leaving a 1½" (3.8cm) opening for turning the pocket (**Figure 6**).

9 Turn the pocket right-side out. Fold the edges of the opening ¼" (6mm) to the inside of the pocket and press (**Figure 7**).

10 Place the pockets in the desired location on the right side of the skirt. Pin them in place. Topstitch down the sides and bottoms close to the edges, leaving the tops open. Be sure to close the bottoms of the pockets in the stitching. Secure the ends with backstitching (**Figure 8**).

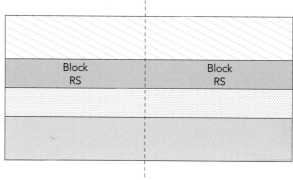

Figure 5

Pocket front RS up under pocket back

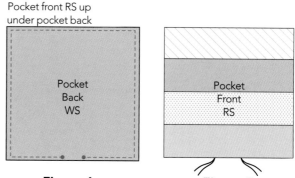

Figure 6   Figure 7

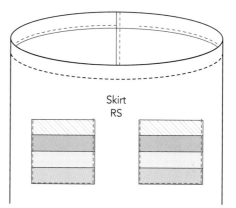

Figure 8

TIP

UNDERSTANDING VALUE

When selecting fabrics, remember that value (the lightness and darkness of a fabric) is just as important as the color itself. By careful manipulation of the colors, patterns and values used in a quilt, you can create depth and interest. The most striking quilts are often the ones that include colors in a variety of tints and shades.

RAIL FENCE QUILT

Finished Dimensions: 64" × 64" (162.6cm × 162.6cm)

MATERIALS

1⅞ yards (1.7m) black fabric (see Note)

1⅞ yards (1.7m) pink fabric (see Note)

1⅞ yards (1.7m) white fabric (see Note)

4⅛ yards (3.8m) backing fabric

¾ yards (0.7m) binding fabric

Matching thread

70" (177.8cm) square (optional)

Note: You can use a single fabric or multiple fabrics of the same color for each yardage requirement. The quilt shown uses 6 black fabrics, 6 pink fabrics and 6 white fabrics.

CUTTING INSTRUCTIONS

Black Fabric
Cut (16) 2½" (6.4cm) strips from selvage edge to selvage edge

Pink Fabric
Cut (16) 2½" (6.4cm) strips from selvage edge to selvage edge

White Fabric
Cut (16) 2½" (6.4cm) strips from selvage edge to selvage edge

---

A LITTLE SLICE OF HEAVEN

I finally started sewing in my late twenties when my mom dragged me to a quilting class. From the moment I walked through the door of the store, I was hooked! I loved all the possibilities that the colors, patterns and textures of the fabrics held, and I found that quilting was something I really enjoyed doing. But then something happened: I had a little girl. With her birth a new world opened up to me: sewing clothing for girls! Again, I was hooked. There is something special about making clothing for my daughters that I will never get tired of. Seeing them wear and enjoy something they helped me make is a little slice of heaven, and I'm thankful for every opportunity I have to sew for them.

— liZ

8½"
(21.6cm)

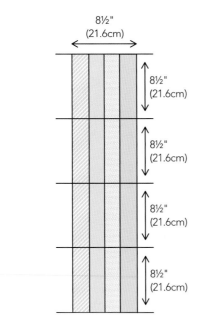

8½"
(21.6cm)

8½"
(21.6cm)

8½"
(21.6cm)

8½"
(21.6cm)

Figure 1

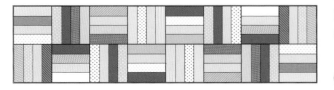

Figure 2

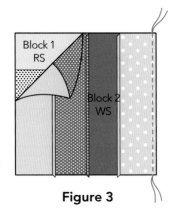

Figure 3

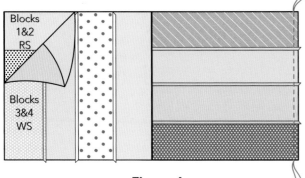

Figure 4

1 Make 64 Rail Fence quilt blocks measuring 8½" (21.6cm) square, following the directions at the beginning of the chapter. The easiest way to do this is to make 16 sets of Rail Fence strip sets and cut each strip set into four 8½" (21.6cm) squares (**Figure 1**).

2 Arrange the quilt into 8 rows of 8 blocks, alternating the direction of every other block (**Figure 2**). Place the blocks randomly.

3 Starting in row 1, place the second block on top of the first, right sides together. Sew the right side seam with a ¼" (6mm) seam allowance (**Figure 3**).

4 Continue sewing block pairs together in the first row, joining blocks 3 and 4, 5 and 6, and 7 and 8. Press all of the seams in row 1 in the same direction.

5 Place the blocks 3 and 4 unit on top of the blocks 1 and 2 unit, right sides together, aligning the seams. Sew the right side seam with a ¼" (6mm) seam allowance (**Figure 4**).

6 Continue joining the block units across the row, aligning the seams and sewing with a ¼" (6mm) seam allowance.

7 Join the blocks in each remaining row following steps 3–6.

8 Place row 2 on top of row 1, right sides together and join with a ¼" (6mm) seam allowance. Repeat to join rows 3 and 4, rows 5 and 6 and rows 7 and 8.

9 Join the sets of rows to complete the quilt top: Place rows 3 and 4 on top of rows 1 and 2, right sides together, and join with a ¼" (6mm) seam allowance. Join rows 5 and 6 to rows 7 and 8 in the same way. Finally, place both halves of the quilt top right sides together and join with a ¼" (6mm) seam allowance. Square the quilt top to 64" (162.6cm).

10 Assemble the quilt back to make a 70" (177.8cm) square backing. For backing instructions, see Chapter 1.

11 Baste and quilt following the instructions in Chapter 1. Alternatively, you can send your quilt out to a long-arm quilter for finishing.

12 Using your binding fabric, bind the quilt as shown in Chapter 1.

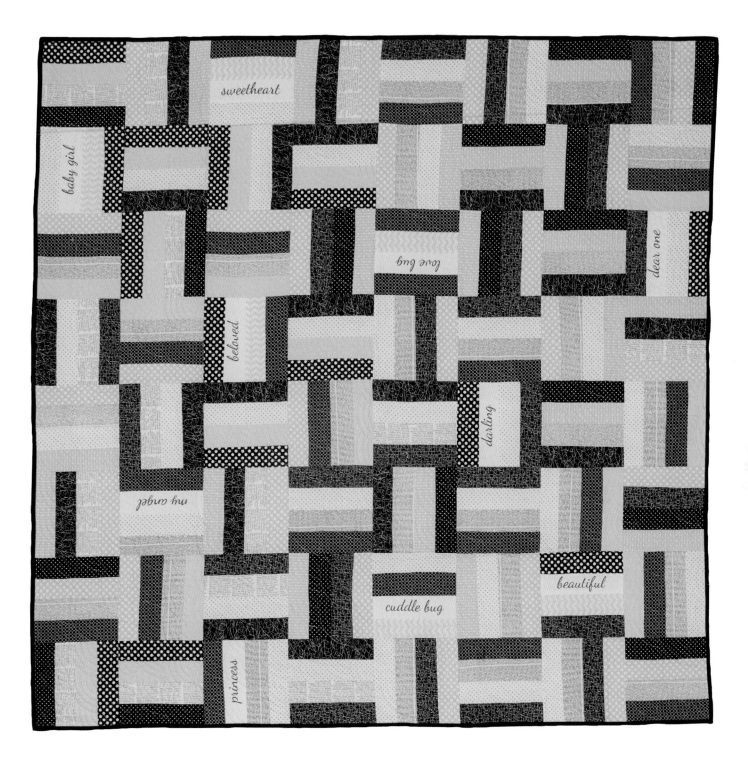

Chapter Six
THE FLYING GEESE

The Flying Geese quilt block can trace its origins back to the early 1800s. During this era, inexpensive cottons began to be printed and became available for use by the general population. This availability of prints led to the rise of many quilt blocks that are still popular today, including the Flying Geese block.

The Flying Geese quilt block is actually a rectangle rather than a square. It is comprised of one large triangle (the goose) surrounded by two smaller triangles (the sky). Traditionally, these blocks are twice as wide as they are tall and once they are completed, they are usually sewn together into long strips with all the triangles facing the same direction. When these strips are completed and stitched together to form a quilt, they do indeed look like a gaggle of geese following one another in a straight line!

How to Make a Flying Geese Quilt Block

These instructions will make a 3" × 6" (7.6cm × 15.2cm) finished block. You'll need two different fabrics for this block and a removable fabric marker.

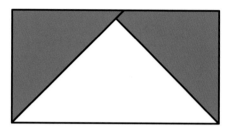

CUTTING INSTRUCTIONS

Main Fabric
Cut (1) 6⅝" × 3⅝" (16.8cm × 9.2cm) rectangle

Background Fabric
Cut (2) 3⅝" (9.2cm) squares

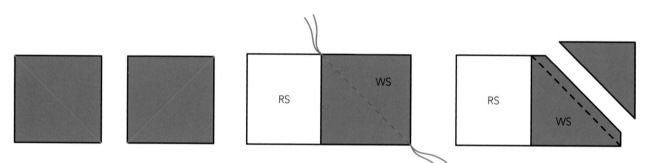

1 On the wrong side of one of the background squares, draw a line from the top left corner to the bottom right corner.

On the second background square, draw a line from the top right corner to the bottom left corner.

2 Place the first square (line going from upper left to lower right) on top of the main rectangle, right sides together. Align the right edges, then stitch down the line drawn on the square.

3 Using a quilting ruler and rotary cutter, trim the excess fabric, leaving a ¼" (6mm) seam allowance. Press the seam on the wrong side away from the goose.

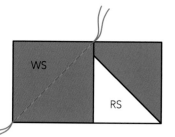

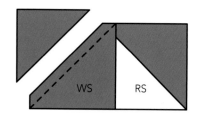

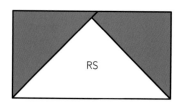

4 Place the second square (line going from upper right to lower left) on the left side of the rectangle, right sides together. Align the edges, then stitch down the line drawn on the square.

5 Trim the block as in step 3, leaving a ¼" (6mm) seam allowance. Press the seam on the wrong side away from the goose.

6 Square up your block so it measures 3½" × 6½" (8.9cm × 16.5cm) following the instructions in Chapter 1. When you sew the block into a project, you will have a 3" × 6" (7.6cm × 15.2cm) finished block.

THE BUS QUILT

I spent countless hours of my youth wrapped in something called the "Bus Quilt." The Bus Quilt was made during a time when my grandparents drove a blue Volkswagen bus with a rainbow painted down the side. It looked really cool but unfortunately had no heat. Because our winters are cold, Grandma made a quilt to stay inside the van. They sold the van shortly after I was born but the quilt remained with my grandparents.

Over the decades that followed, the Bus Quilt became a part of almost every visit with my grandparents. We used it to snuggle in during movies, curl up underneath during sleepovers, build forts with and wrap us up when we were sick. That quilt, with its crazy colors and shapes, has become a family treasure. It's hard to believe that a single handmade item can hold so many memories for so many people. All it takes is one look to bring back a flood of memories that tie my siblings, cousins and I together with endless card games, trips to the beach and family vacations. Because of this we are all bound together by the love that we shared over the years that my grandparents employed the use of the Bus Quilt. Little did my grandma know years and years ago when she tied that quilt she would be creating something that would tie her family together for generations to come.

— liz

FLYING GEESE ZIPPER POUCH

Makes one 8½" × 11½" (21.6cm × 29.2cm) pouch

MATERIALS

⅓ yard (0.3m) main fabric

⅓ yard (0.3m) lining fabric

¼ yard (0.2m) Flying Geese triangle fabric

¼ yard (0.2m) Flying Geese background fabric

9" (22.9cm) zipper

⅓ yard (0.3m) fusible fleece

Matching thread

Zipper foot (for sewing machine)

Yarn for pom-pom

CUTTING INSTRUCTIONS

Flying Geese Triangle Fabric
Cut (5) 2¼" × 4" (5.7cm × 10.2cm) rectangles

Flying Geese Background Fabric
Cut (10) 2¼" (5.7cm) squares

Main
Cut (1) 9¼" × 12" (23.5cm × 30.5cm) rectangle (back)
Cut (1) 2" × 9¼" (5.1cm × 23.5cm) rectangle (front 1)
Cut (1) 7" × 9¼" (17.8cm × 23.5cm) rectangle (front 2)
Cut (2) 2" × 4" (5.1cm × 10.2cm) rectangles (zipper)

Lining Fabric
Cut (2) 9¼" × 12" (23.5cm × 30.5cm) rectangles

Fusible Fleece
Cut (2) 9¼" × 12" (23.5cm × 30.5cm) rectangles

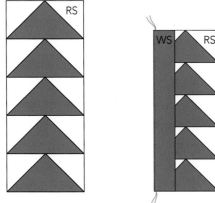

Figure 1

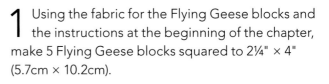

Figure 2

Figure 3

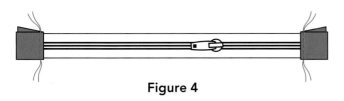

Figure 4

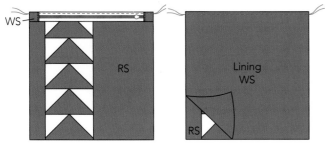

Figure 5   **Figure 6**

1 Using the fabric for the Flying Geese blocks and the instructions at the beginning of the chapter, make 5 Flying Geese blocks squared to 2¼" × 4" (5.7cm × 10.2cm).

2 Stitch the Flying Geese blocks into a single column, using a ¼" (6mm) seam allowance (**Figure 1**). Alternate pressing the seams up and down.

3 Place the front 1 rectangle on top of the Flying Geese strip, right sides together, aligning the left edges. Pin in place and stitch the pieces together with a ¼" (6mm) seam allowance (**Figure 2**). Press the seam toward the solid fabric

4 Place the front 2 rectangle on the other side of the Flying Geese strip, right sides together, aligning the right edges. Pin in place and stitch with a ¼" (6mm) seam allowance (**Figure 3**). Press the seam toward the solid fabric.

5 Following the manufacturer's directions, fuse 1 piece of fusible fleece to the wrong side of the completed pouch front piece. Press the second piece of fusible fleece to the wrong side of the pouch back piece.

6 Press both of the 2" × 4" (5.1cm × 10.2cm) rectangles in half so that they are 2" (5.1cm) squares. Place the folded edges of the squares over the ends of the zipper and stitch in place using a zipper foot (**Figure 4**).

7 Place the zipper along the top edge of the pouch front, right sides together, and baste in place using a zipper foot (**Figure 5**). Lay the lining piece on top of the pouch and zipper, right-side down. Pin the pieces together. Stitch along the top edge of the pouch, sewing through all 3 layers (**Figure 6**).

8 Turn the lining piece to the inside and press well. Topstitch the lining in place.

9 Repeat steps 7 and 8 to attach the back pouch piece and remaining lining piece to the other side of the zipper (**Figure 7**).

10 Open the zipper a few inches (about 8cm). With the zipper in the middle, running top to bottom, pull the front and back main pouch pieces to the left and align the raw edges, right sides together. Pin in place. Pull the lining pieces to the right, right sides together. Align the raw edges and pin.

Sew around the perimeter of the pouch with a ¼" (6mm) seam allowance. Leave a 2" (5.1cm) opening in the lining (**Figure 8**).

11 Turn the pouch right-side out, pushing all the fabric through the 2" (5.1cm) opening.

12 Hand stitch or machine stitch the 2" (5.1cm) opening in the lining closed (**Figure 9**), then push the lining inside the bag through the zipper opening.

13 Create a pom-pom by wrapping yarn around the tines of a fork 15 to 20 times. Cut a small piece of yarn and tie it tightly around the middle of the wrapped yarn. Cut the looped ends of the pom-pom and trim to create a circular shape. Leave the ends of the middle tie piece long and use them to tie the pom-pom onto the zipper pull.

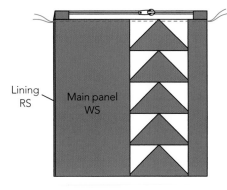

Lining RS

Main panel WS

Figure 7

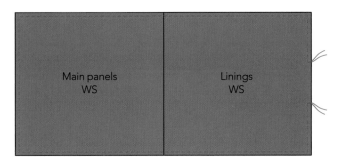

Main panels WS

Linings WS

Figure 8

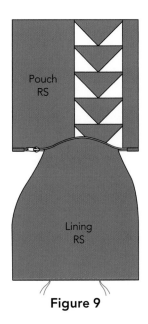

Pouch RS

Lining RS

Figure 9

FLYING GEESE QUILT

Finished Dimensions: 49" × 53½" (124.5cm × 135.9cm)

MATERIALS

½ yard (0.5m) each of 6 different print fabrics

3 yards (2.7m) background fabric

4 yards (3.7m) backing fabric

Matching thread

66" (167.6cm) square of batting

7 yards (6.4m) of prepared binding

Basting spray (optional)

Walking foot (for sewing machine; optional)

CUTTING INSTRUCTIONS

Print Fabrics
Cut (6) 3⅝" × 6⅝" (9.2cm × 16.8cm) rectangles from each fabric (36 rectangles total)

Background Fabric
Cut (72) 3⅝" (9.2cm) squares

Cut (12) 3½" (8.9cm) squares

Cut (12) 3½" × 6½" (8.9cm × 16.5cm) rectangles

Cut (1) 24½" × 54½" (62.2cm × 138.4cm) rectangle

Cut (1) 9½" × 54½" (24.1cm × 138.4cm) rectangle

> *"It isn't the shape of the designs or the points or the batting, it's the love you sew into your quilt that is your true legacy."*
>
> —Lisa Boyer

1 Make 36 Flying Geese blocks using the 3⅝" × 6⅝" (9.2cm × 16.8cm) print rectangles and the 3⅝" (9.2cm) background squares. Follow the directions at the beginning of the chapter if you need help making the blocks. Square the blocks to 3½" × 6½" (8.9cm × 16.5cm) if necessary.

2 Create a large Flying Geese block unit. Lay out 6 Flying Geese blocks, two 3½" × 6½" (8.9cm × 16.5cm) background rectangles and two 3½" (8.9cm) background squares following the layout in **Figure 1**.

3 Assemble the first row of the block unit: Lay the Flying Geese block on top of the background rectangle, right sides together, and sew the right side seam with a ¼" (6mm) seam allowance. Stitch the second background rectangle to the other side of the Flying Geese block, right sides together, with a ¼" (6mm) seam allowance. Press the seams toward the background blocks.

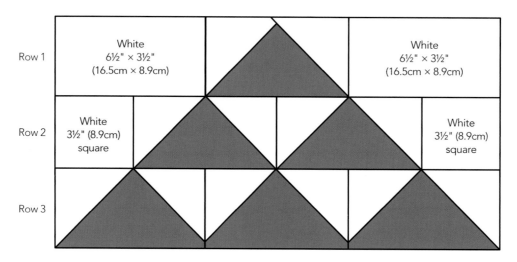

Figure 1

4 Join the blocks in the second row in the same manner, sewing with a ¼" (6mm) seam allowance and pressing the seams toward the middle. Press the center seam in either direction.

5 Join the blocks in the third row, stitching with a ¼" (6mm) seam allowance. Press the seams toward the outer blocks.

6 Join the 3 rows, stitching with a ¼" (6mm) seam allowance. Nest the seams as described in Chapter 1.

7 Repeat steps 2–6 to make 5 more large Flying Geese block units. Square up each of the large units to 9½"× 18½" (24.1cm × 47cm), as described in Chapter 1.

8 Lay out all 6 large Flying Geese units in a column. Join the blocks one at a time, right sides together, sewing with a ¼" (6mm) seam allowance (**Figure 2**). Press the seams all in one direction, either all up or all down.

9 Place the 9½" × 54½" (24.1cm × 138.4cm) strip on the left side of the Flying Geese strip, right sides together. Align the left edges and pin in place. Stitch the seam with a ¼" (6mm) seam allowance (**Figure 3**). Press the seam toward the darker fabric.

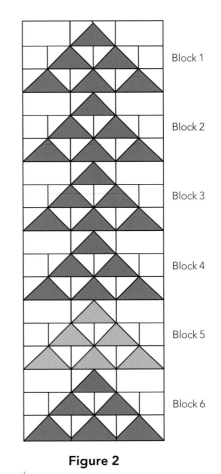

Block 1

Block 2

Block 3

Block 4

Block 5

Block 6

Figure 2

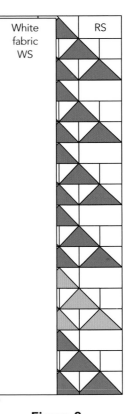

White fabric WS

RS

Figure 3

10 Place the 24½" × 54½" (62.2cm × 138.4cm) piece on the opposite side of the Flying Geese panel, right sides together. Align the right edges and pin. Sew the seam with a ¼" (6mm) seam allowance (**Figure 4**). Press the seam to the outside.

11 Square up your quilt top to 49½" × 54" (125.7cm × 137.2cm) using the method described in Chapter 1.

12 Prepare a quilt backing 56" × 60" (142.2cm × 152.4cm), using the method in Chapter 1. If you plan on sending your quilt to a long-arm quilter, you're done!

13 If you are basting and quilting your quilt yourself, follow the methods described in Chapter 1.

14 Bind your quilt using the prepared binding. See Chapter 1 for more details.

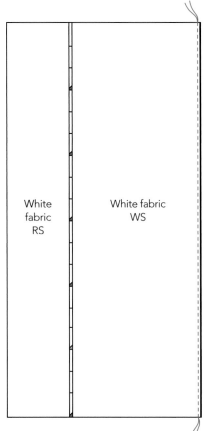

Figure 4

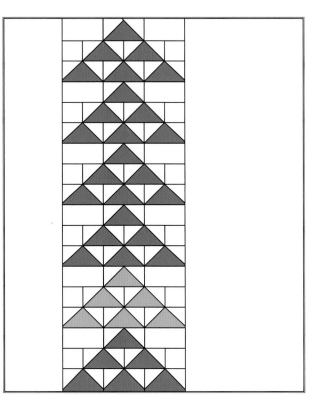

Finished Quilt Top

Chapter Seven
THE LOG CABIN

The history of the Log Cabin quilt block is most strongly associated with frontier life in the mid-1800s. In reality, the Log Cabin design was probably first used to make quilts in England in the early 1800s but the block's popularity exploded with the westward expansion of the United States. There, women turned hand-dyed scraps into masterpieces and Log Cabin quilts became a staple in their homes.

The Log Cabin block gets its name from the narrow strips that surround the square in the middle of the block. However, the block itself represents much more than just a dwelling. To the women who created these blocks, they symbolized home, family, love and security. Traditionally, the square in the middle of the block was red to represent the heart and hearth of the home.

The Log Cabin design has survived decades of changes, trends and technologies. From the Amish women's bold two-color version that modern quilters still love today to the velvet and satin versions of the Victorian Age, the Log Cabin block has proved to be an enduring quilt block for women of any generation.

How to Make a Log Cabin Quilt Block

There are many different variations and configurations of the Log Cabin block; however, all of them are made with a square surrounded by strips of fabric. This is an example of a classic 12½" (31.8cm) Log Cabin quilt block.

Traditionally, these blocks were made by stitching scrap strips around the center block. In this chapter, the blocks are made from pieces cut to exact measurements. You can use a variety of different fabrics to make your blocks. Use each fabric once in the block, or repeat fabrics throughout the block. Get creative with your combinations!

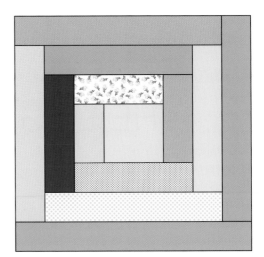

CUTTING INSTRUCTIONS

A: Cut a 3½" (8.9cm) square

B: Cut a 3½" × 2" (8.9cm × 5.1cm) strip

C: Cut a 5" × 2" (12.7cm × 5.1cm) strip

D: Cut a 5" × 2" (12.7cm × 5.1cm) strip

E: Cut a 6½" × 2" (16.5cm × 5.1cm) strip

F: Cut a 6½" × 2" (16.5cm × 5.1cm) strip

G: Cut an 8" × 2" (20.3cm × 5.1cm) strip

H: Cut an 8" × 2" (20.3cm × 5.1cm) strip

I: Cut a 9½" × 2" (24.1cm × 5.1cm) strip

J: Cut a 9½" × 2" (24.1cm × 5.1cm) strip

K: Cut an 11" × 2" (27.9cm × 5.1cm) strip

L: Cut an 11" × 2" (27.9cm × 5.1cm) strip

M: Cut a 12½" × 2" (31.8cm × 5.1cm) strip

TIP

TYPES OF FABRICS

When you begin quilting, we suggest you work with 100% cotton quilting cottons. These fabrics are long lasting, handle well and withstand washing. After you become comfortable with sewing and quilting, experiment with a wider variety of fabrics (some of which can be just as fussy to work with as they are beautiful to look at!).

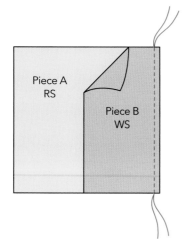

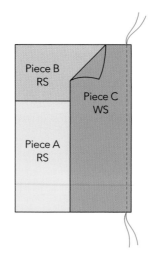

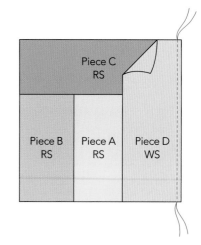

1 Place piece B on top of piece A, right sides together. Stitch the side seam with a ¼" (6mm) seam allowance. Open the pieces and press the seam on the back side toward piece B.

2 Place piece C on top of the AB unit, right sides together. Stitch the side seam with a ¼" (6mm) seam allowance. Open the pieces and press the seam on the back side toward piece C.

3 Place piece D on top of pieces A and C, right sides together. Stitch the side seam with a ¼" (6mm) seam allowance. Open the pieces and press the seam on the back side toward piece D.

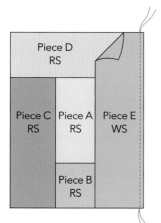

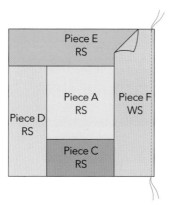

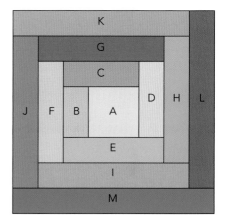

4 Place piece E on top of pieces D, A and B, right sides together. Stitch the side seam with a ¼" (6mm) seam allowance. Open the pieces and press the seam on the back side toward piece E.

5 Place piece F on top of pieces E, B and C, right sides together. Stitch the side seam with a ¼" (6mm) seam allowance. Open the pieces and press the seam on the back side toward piece F.

6 Continue this same process, working clockwise around the block (in alphabetical order, following the block map above) until your quilt block is finished.

LOG CABIN FRAMED BLOCK

Makes one 12" (30.5cm) block

MATERIALS

⅛ yard (11cm) of 5 different fabrics (scraps are fine)

13" (33cm) square of all-cotton batting (optional)

Removable fabric marker (optional)

Matching thread

Walking foot (for sewing machine; optional)

12" (30.5cm) picture frame

Basting spray (optional)

CUTTING INSTRUCTIONS

Fabric 1
Cut (1) 4½" (11.4cm) square (piece A)

Fabric 2
Cut (2) 4½" × 2½" (11.4cm × 6.4cm) pieces (pieces B and C)

Fabric 3
Cut (2) 8½" × 2½" (21.6cm × 6.4cm) pieces (pieces D and E)

Fabric 4
Cut (2) 8½" × 2½" (21.6cm × 6.4cm) pieces (pieces F and G)

Fabric 5
Cut (2) 12½" × 2½" (31.8cm × 6.4cm) pieces (pieces H and I)

COURTHOUSE STEPS

This block is a popular version of the Log Cabin quilt block called "Courthouse Steps." It is a very simple version of the original Log Cabin block but has a modern look and feel.

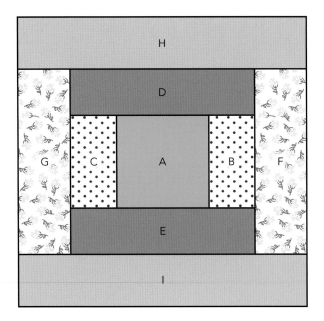

Figure 1

1 Assemble the Log Cabin block using **Figure 1** as a guide: Place piece B on top of piece A, right sides together and aligning the right edges, and stitch with a ¼" (6mm) seam allowance. Open and press the seams toward piece B.

2 Place piece C on top of piece A, right sides together and aligning the left edges, and stitch with a ¼" (6mm) seam allowance. Open and press the seams toward piece C.

3 Place piece D on top of the unit created in steps 1 and 2. Align the top edges, right sides together, and stitch with a ¼" (6mm) seam allowance. Open and press the seams toward piece D.

4 Add piece E to the bottom of the unit, right sides together and aligning the bottom edges. Stitch with a ¼" (6mm) seam allowance. Open and press the seams toward piece E.

5 Continue building the block in this manner, adding pieces F and G to the right and left sides of the block, then adding pieces H and I to the top and bottom of the block. Press.

A CHERISHED TRADITION

It's no small surprise to me that handmade quilts are still given today at momentous occasions in one's life: births, coming of age, marriage, etc. When someone gives you a quilt, they are giving you a tangible piece of their heart, something you can always carry with you, that can bring you comfort and remind you that someone cares. What better time is there to wrap someone with your love than when celebrating a precious addition to a family, mourning the loss of a loved one, beginning a new life or fighting an illness? Quilts are always an appropriate and appreciated token of our love, and I believe they will continue to be a cherished tradition for generations to come.

— liz

6 If you'd like to quilt your square, do so now (if not, skip ahead to step 8). Draw lines onto the block using a removable marker. Baste your quilt block onto the batting using basting spray. Start with a line from corner to corner on the bias, then continue to work out, drawing diagonal lines ½" (1.3cm) apart. Repeat in the opposite direction to create a crosshatch pattern (**Figure 2**).

7 With your walking foot on your sewing machine, quilt down the lines you've just drawn.

8 Square your block to 12" (30.5cm) following the directions in Chapter 1.

9 Frame your block and hang, if desired (**Figure 3**).

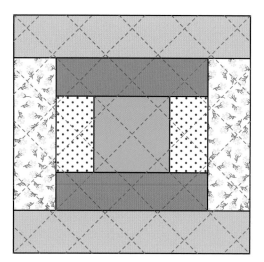

Figure 2

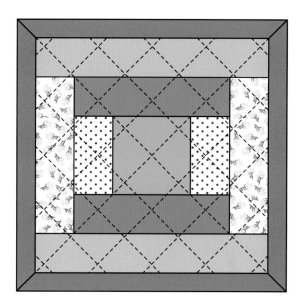

Figure 3

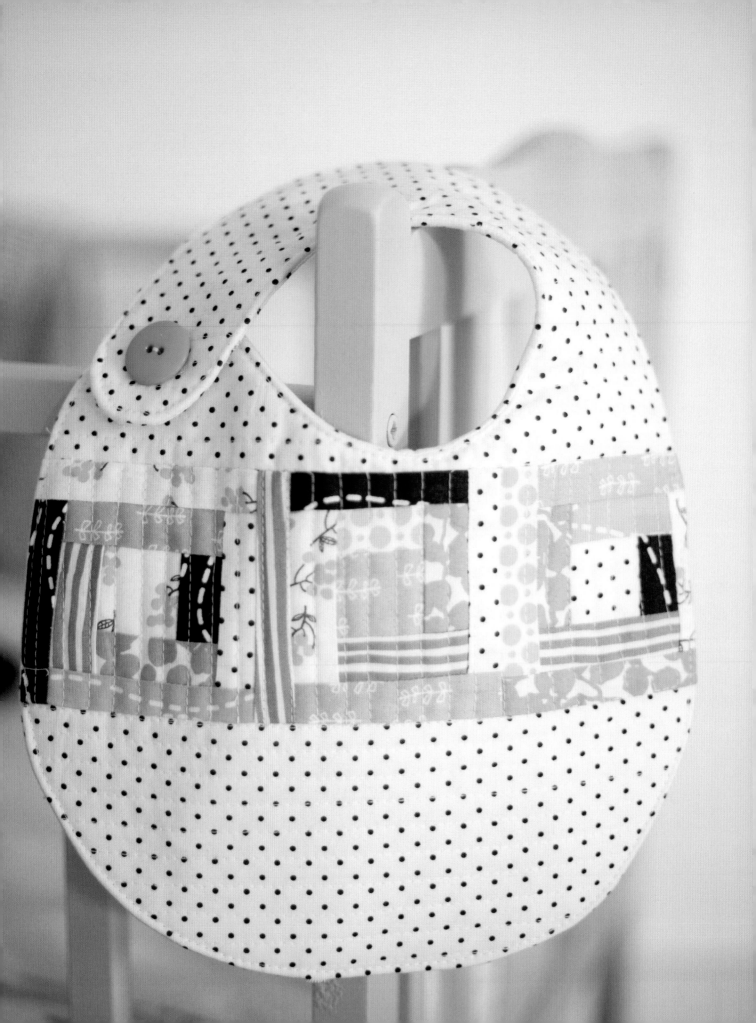

LOG CABIN BABY BIB

Makes one bib

MATERIALS

½ yard (0.5m) Swiss dot fabric

Leftover pieces of coordinating fabric from the *Log Cabin Quilt* or other fabric scraps

12" × 14" (30.5cm × 35.6cm) piece of all-cotton batting

12" × 14" (30.5cm × 35.6cm) piece of cotton backing fabric

Removable fabric marker

1–2" (2.5–5.1cm) length of sewable hook-and-loop tape

1 button (optional, see Note)

Walking foot (for sewing machine)

Matching thread

Basting spray

Bib pattern (see Templates)

Note: The button is for decorative purposes only and could potentially cause a choking hazard. Please use at your own discretion.

CUTTING INSTRUCTIONS

Swiss Dot Fabric
Cut (1) bib back, (1) each of the bib front pieces

Piece 1
Cut (3) 1½" (3.8cm) squares

Piece 2
Cut (3) 1" × 1½" (2.5cm × 3.8cm) rectangles

Piece 3
Cut (3) 1" × 2" (2.5cm × 5.1cm) rectangles

Piece 4
Cut (3) 1" × 2" (2.5cm × 5.1cm) rectangles

Piece 5
Cut (3) 1" × 2½" (2.5cm × 6.4cm) rectangles

Piece 6
Cut (3) 1" × 2½" (2.5cm × 6.4cm) rectangles

Piece 7
Cut (3) 1" × 3" (2.5cm × 7.6cm) rectangles

Piece 8
Cut (3) 1" × 3" (2.5cm × 7.6cm) rectangles

Piece 9
Cut (3) 1" × 3½" (2.5cm × 8.9cm) rectangles

TIP

CHOKING HAZARD

Buttons are a choking hazard for children under the age of three. Consider using velcro instead.

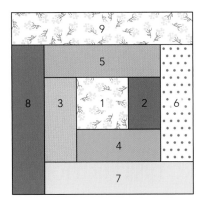

Figure 1

1 Follow the Log Cabin block directions at the beginning of this chapter to make three 3" (7.6cm) quilt blocks. Use **Figure 1** as a guide.

2 Place 2 of the quilt blocks right sides together and stitch the side with a ¼" (6mm) seam allowance. Lay the third quilt block on top of the second, right sides together, aligning the right edges. Join with a ¼" (6mm) seam allowance (**Figure 2**). Press all seams to one side.

3 Align the block unit with the edge of bib front piece 1, right sides together, and pin in place. Stitch with a ¼" (6mm) seam allowance (**Figure 3**). Open the pieces and press the seam away from the blocks.

4 Align the other side of the block unit with the edge of bib front piece 2, right sides together, and pin in place. Stitch with a ¼" (6mm) seam allowance (**Figure 4**). Open the pieces and press the seam away from the blocks.

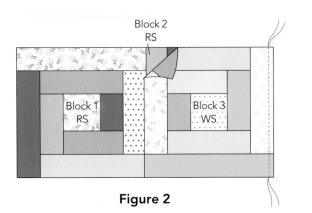

Figure 2

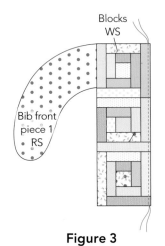

Figure 3

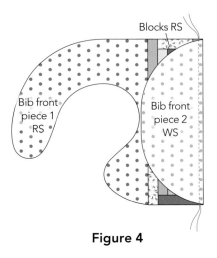

Figure 4

5 Mark vertical lines down your bib front, ½" (1.3cm) apart, using a removable marker (**Figure 5**).

6 Baste your bib top to the batting with basting spray following the instructions in Chapter 1.

7 With your walking foot on your sewing machine, stitch on the drawn lines. Trim the excess batting from the bib.

8 Pin the bib back to the bib front, right sides together (**Figure 6**).

9 Stitch around the edge of the bib with a ¼" (6mm) seam allowance, stopping about 2" (5.1cm) before you reach your starting point. Clip the curves, being careful not to clip through the stitches.

10 Turn the bib right-side out through the 2" (5.1cm) opening and press. Turn the edges of the opening under, and topstitch around the edges of the bib. This will close the 2" (5.1cm) opening (**Figure 7**).

11 Stitch the hook-and-loop tape in place on the front and back of the bib. If you want to add a button, stitch it securely on the right side of the bib top above the hook-and-loop tape.

"Blankets wrap you in warmth,
quilts wrap you in love."

—Anonymous

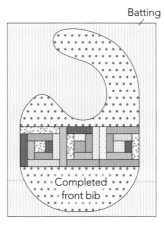

Figure 5

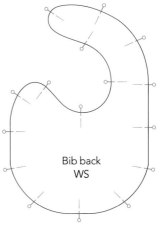

Figure 6

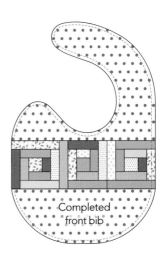

Figure 7

LOG CABIN QUILT

Finished Dimensions: 40" × 40" (101.6cm × 101.6cm)

MATERIALS

½ yard (0.5m) each of 7 different fabrics

1¼ yards (1.1m) all-cotton batting

1¼ yards (1.1m) backing fabric

½ yard (0.5m) binding fabric

Matching thread

Removable fabric marker

Walking foot (for sewing machine)

44" (111.8cm) square of batting

Note: This fabric amount is enough to make all three projects in this chapter, as the other two projects are made mostly of scraps.

CUTTING INSTRUCTIONS

Fabric 1
Cut (1) 10½" (26.7cm) square (piece A)

Fabric 2
Cut (1) 10½" × 5½" (26.7cm × 14cm) strip (piece B)

Cut (1) 30½" × 5½" (77.5cm × 14cm) strip (piece J)

Fabric 3
Cut (1) 15½" × 5½" (39.4cm × 14cm) strip (piece C)

Fabric 4
Cut (1) 15½" × 5½" (39.4cm × 14cm) strip (piece D)

Cut (1) 35½" × 5½" (90.2cm × 14cm) strip (piece L)

Fabric 5
Cut (1) 20½" × 5½" (52.1cm × 14cm) strip (piece E)

Cut (1) 30½" × 5½" (77.5cm × 14cm) strip (piece K)

Fabric 6
Cut (1) 20½" × 5½" (52.1cm × 14cm) strip (piece F)

Fabric 7
Cut (1) 25½" × 5½" (64.8cm × 14cm) strip (piece G)

Cut (1) 40½" × 5½" (10.29cm × 14cm) strip (piece M)

Fabric 8
Cut (1) 30" × 5½" (76.2cm × 14cm) strip (piece I)

Fabric 9
Cut (1) 25½" × 5½" (64.8cm × 14cm) strip (piece H)

THE GARAGE SALE QUILT

Several years ago while out shopping garage sales with my mom, I peered into a box and found an old quilt. Not just any old quilt, a hand-pieced yo-yo quilt with hundreds (I dare say thousands) of yo-yos on it. I had tried my hand at yo-yo making a time or two, but I think the most I ever got to was ten or so before I had given up. I fully understood the work that had gone into this quilt. In my heart, I knew someone had spent many, many precious hours on those yo-yos and that it needed to be cherished and preserved. So, I paid thirty dollars for the king-sized quilt and took it home where I carefully hand washed it and hung it to dry.

I love that quilt and often use it to teach students about the relationship between quilting and life. I explain how a yo-yo is made, how tedious the process is, then hold up that amazing quilt with all its yo-yos. Usually the students' eyes get big. They understand the hours and hours of work that went into that quilt.

Then I talk about the individual yo-yos, how some are dark and dingy (probably once a worn-out pair of pants) and how others are bright and cheery. I talk about life and how some days are dark and dingy and others are bright and cheery, but how all those days, or hours, or minutes became this wonderful quilt.

— Elizabeth

1 This quilt is assembled as one large Log Cabin quilt block. Use the cutting chart and **Figure 1** to lay out your pieces.

2 Align the long edge of piece 2 with the edge of piece 1, right sides together. Sew the pieces together with a ¼" (6mm) side seam (**Figure 2**). Open the pieces and press the seam toward the dark fabric.

3 Continue assembling your block 1 piece at a time following the directions at the beginning of this chapter. Use **Figure 1** as a guide when assembling.

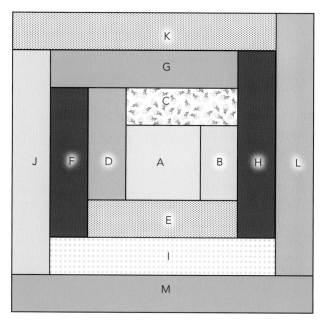

Figure 1

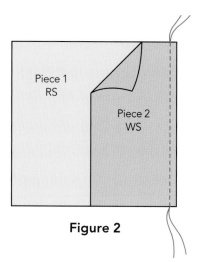

Figure 2

4 Baste your quilt top using any of the methods described in Chapter 1.

5 With a removable marker, draw vertical lines on your quilt top, 1" (2.5cm) apart.

6 Use your walking foot to stitch down each of the marked lines.

7 Trim the quilt to 40" (101.6cm) square. Bind the quilt using the instructions in Chapter 1.

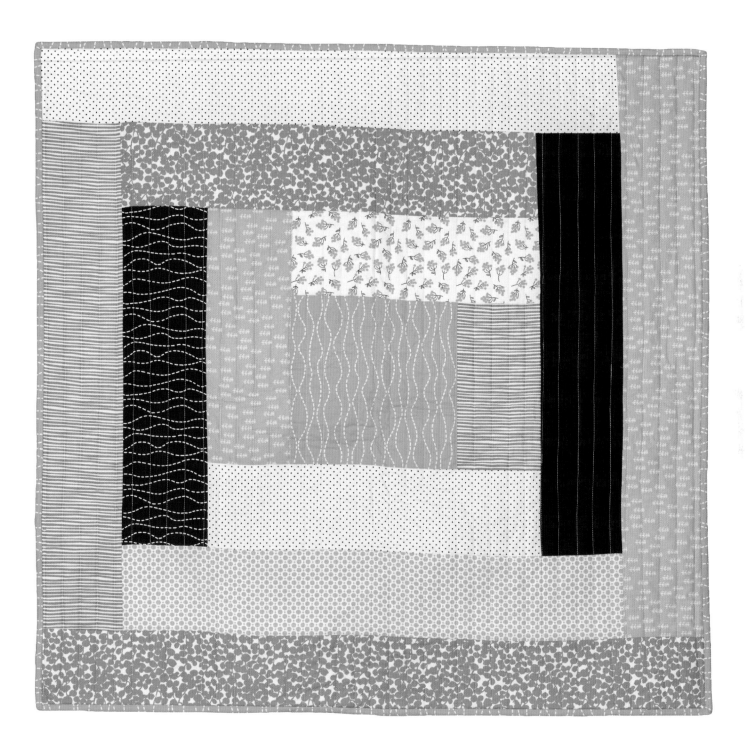

Chapter Eight
THE OHIO STAR

While the origins of the Ohio Star quilt block can be traced back to the early 1800s, its rise to popularity didn't come until the 1930s. At that time during the Depression and post-Depression eras, the design was rediscovered by a new generation of quilters: especially Scottish and Irish immigrants, as well as the Amish.

The Ohio Star is another block that is known by several different names, such as the Variable Star and the Texas Star. Like so many other blocks, it is just a set variation of a standard Nine Patch quilt block, this one being comprised of five solid blocks and four hourglass blocks.

How to Make an Ohio Star Quilt Block

These instructions will make a 21" (53.3cm) finished block. You'll need four different fabrics for this block and a removable fabric marker.

CUTTING INSTRUCTIONS

Fabric 1 (stripes)
Cut (8) 4½" (11.4cm) squares

Fabric 2 (dots)
Cut (4) 4½" (11.4cm) squares

Fabric 3 (floral)
Cut (4) 4½" (11.4cm) squares
Cut (1) 7½" (19.1cm) square

Fabric 4 (solid)
Cut (4) 7½" (19.1cm) squares

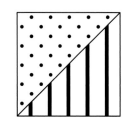

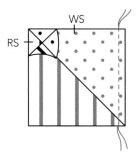

1 Using 4 striped squares and 4 dotted squares, follow the directions at the beginning of Chapter 3 and make 8 Half-Square Triangles. Square each half-square block to 4" (10.2cm).

2 Place a stripe/dot unit on top of a stripe/dot unit, right sides together. Make sure the stripes are on top of the stripes and the dots are on top of the dots. Sew along the dominantly dotted side with a ¼" (6mm) seam allowance.

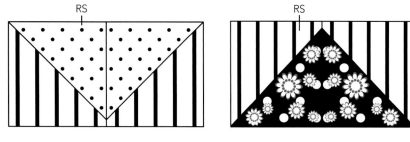

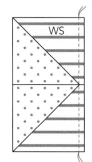

3 Repeat steps 1 and 2 using the remaining striped squares and the 4½" (11.4cm) floral squares. When you're finished, you'll have 4 stripe/dot units and 4 floral/stripe units.

4 Place a stripe/dot unit on top of a floral/stripe unit, right sides together. Make sure the stripes are on top of the stripes and the dots are on top of the floral. Sew along the dominantly striped side with a ¼" (6mm) seam allowance.

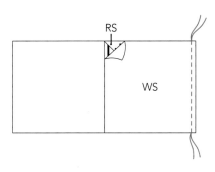

5 Press the seam open and square the block to 7½" (19.1cm). Repeat steps 4 and 5 until you have 4 blocks like the one above.

6 Lay out your completed blocks along with the four 7½" (19.1cm) solid squares and the 7½" (19.1cm) floral square, using the illustration above as a guide.

7 Sew row 1 of the Ohio Star block, joining the squares one at a time with a ¼" (6mm) seam allowance and pressing the seams to the dark side.

Join the blocks in rows 2 and 3 in the same fashion, sewing them with a ¼" (6mm) seam allowance. Press the seams open.

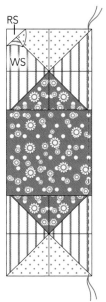

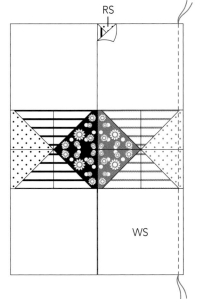

8 Place row 2 on top of row 1, right sides together, and stitch down the side with a ¼" (6mm) seam allowance. Press the seam open.

9 Place row 3 on top of row 2, right sides together, and stitch down the side with a ¼" (6mm) seam allowance. Press open.

10 Square the block to 21½" (54.6cm).

OHIO STAR PILLOW

Makes one 18" (45.7cm) square pillow

MATERIALS

¼ yard (23cm) of white with black Swiss dot fabric (Fabric 1)

¼ yard (23cm) of black and white stripe fabric (Fabric 2)

½ yard (0.5m) of black with white Swiss dot fabric (Fabric 3)

¼ yard (23cm) floral on black polka dot fabric (Fabric 4)

Matching thread

18" (45.7cm) pillow form

CUTTING INSTRUCTIONS

Fabric 1 (white with black Swiss dot)
Cut (8) 2" (5.1cm) squares
Cut (1) 2½" (6.4cm) square

Fabric 2 (stripes)
Cut (8) 2" (5.1cm) squares

Fabric 3 (black with white Swiss dot)
Cut (4) 2½" (6.4cm) squares
Cut (2) 7" (17.8cm) squares
Cut (2) 14" × 18" (35.6cm × 45.7cm) pieces

Fabric 4 (floral on white)
Cut (4) 6½" (16.5cm) squares

Fabric 5 (floral on black)
Cut (4) 7" (17.8cm) squares

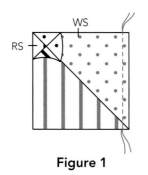

Figure 1

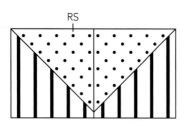

Figure 2

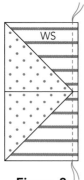

Figure 3

Figure 4

1 Following the instructions at the beginning of Chapter 3, use 8 of the Fabric 1 squares and the 8 Fabric 2 squares to make 16 Half-Square Triangles. Open the blocks, pressing the seams to the dark side. Square the blocks to 1½" (3.8cm).

2 Place 2 Half-Square Triangle blocks on top of each other, right sides together, making sure Fabric 1 is on top of Fabric 1. Sew the right side seam with a ¼" (6mm) seam allowance (**Figure 1**). Press open. Repeat with the remaining Half-Square Triangles. You will have 8 rectangles (**Figure 2**).

3 Place 2 of the rectangle blocks on top of each other, right sides together, Fabric 1 on top of Fabric 1. Stitch the right side seam with a ¼" (6mm) seam allowance (**Figure 3**). Press the finished square open and trim it to 2½" (6.4cm).

4 Repeat step 3 with the remaining rectangle blocks. You will have 4 square blocks total (**Figure 4**).

5 Lay out the blocks from step 4 with the remaining Fabric 1 square and the 2½" (6.4cm) Fabric 3 squares, using **Figure 5** as a guide.

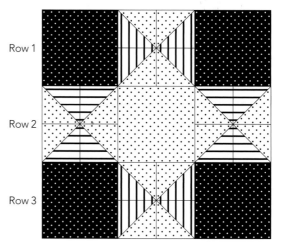

Figure 5

6 Assemble row 1 of the Star block, placing the second square of the row on top of the first square, right sides together. Stitch the right side seam with a ¼" (6mm) seam allowance and press the seam toward the darker fabric.

Join the third square to the second square in the same manner (**Figure 6**). Press the seam to the darker side.

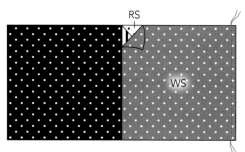

Figure 6

7 Sew the squares in rows 2 and 3 in the same way as described in step 6. Press the seams in each row in the opposite direction.

8 Join the 3 rows of the Ohio Star block. Start by placing the second row on top of the first, right sides together, and pin in place. Sew with a ¼" (6mm) seam allowance (**Figure 7**) and press the seam open.

Join the third row to the second in the same manner. Press the seam open. Square the block to 6½" (16.5cm).

Figure 7

9 Use the 7" (17.8cm) Fabric 3 and Fabric 5 squares to make 4 Half-Square Triangles following the directions at the beginning of Chapter 3. Open each block and press the seam toward the Fabric 5. Square the blocks to 6½" (16.5cm).

10 Lay out the 4 blocks you created in step 9, the Ohio Star block and the 6½" (16.5cm) Fabric 4 squares, using **Figure 8** as a guide.

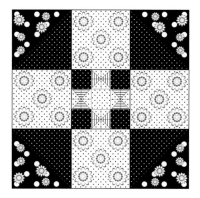

Figure 8

11 Follow steps 6–8 to join the blocks in each row, then join the 3 rows. Your pillow front is now complete.

12 Turn under one long edge ½" (1.3cm) on each of the 14" × 18" (35.6cm × 45.7cm) pieces. Press. Turn the edge on each piece under another ½" (1.3cm) to the wrong side and press. Stitch close to the inner fold.

13 Place one of the back pieces right sides together onto the pillow front, aligning the raw edges, and pin (**Figure 9**). Pin the second back piece to the other end of the pillow front, right sides together. The second back piece will overlap the first on the hemmed edges.

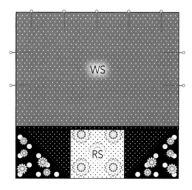

Figure 9

14 Sew around the entire perimeter of the pillow with a ¼" (6mm) seam allowance. Reinforce the corners by stitching twice. Trim the corners at an angle, being careful not to cut the stitches. Turn the cover right-side out and press.

OHIO STAR SEWING MACHINE COVER

Makes one 15½" × 29" (39.4cm × 73.7cm) cover

MATERIALS

⅛ yard (11cm) Swiss dot fabric (Fabric 1)

1 yard (1m) large floral fabric (Fabric 2)

⅛ yard (11cm) small floral fabric (Fabric 3)

¼ yard (23cm) small geometric print fabric (for the binding)

18" × 31" (45.7cm × 78.7cm) of batting

Removable fabric marker (optional)

8" (20.3cm) of 2" (5.1cm)-wide elastic

Walking foot (for sewing machine; optional)

Basting spray (optional)

CUTTING INSTRUCTIONS

Fabric 1 (Swiss dot)
Cut (4) 3" (7.6cm) squares
Cut (1) 4" (10.2cm) square

Fabric 2 (large floral)
Cut (4) 3" (7.6cm) squares
Cut (4) 4" (10.2cm) squares
Cut (1) 2½" × 11" (6.4cm × 27.9cm) strip
Cut (1) 5" × 13¼" (12.7cm × 33.7cm) strip
Cut (1) 15½" × 16½" (39.4cm × 41.9cm) rectangle

Fabric 3 (small floral)
Cut (8) 3" (7.6cm) squares

Elastic
Cut (2) 4" (10.2cm) pieces

QUILT BLOCKS

I am lucky enough to be named after my great-grandmother Elizabeth, who was an excellent quilter. During the summer she would often keep her treadle sewing machine out on the front porch to sew during the long cool evenings. Living on a dairy farm and raising eight kids meant that she didn't have a lot of extra funds for fabric or time for sewing, but what she was able to create out of so little is truly amazing.

Several years ago my mom discovered some loose quilt blocks that my great-grandmother had made and turned them into a beautiful quilt. She framed one of the leftover blocks that now hangs in my sewing room. It reminds me of family, tradition, creativity, frugality and craftsmanship. Coincidentally, that leftover framed block made by my great-grandmother just so happens to be an Ohio Star.

— liZ

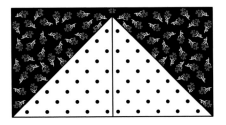

Figure 1
Unit 1; Make 4

Figure 2
Unit 2; Make 4

Figure 3

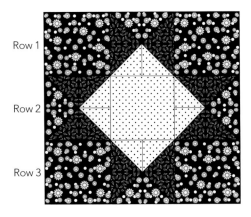

Row 1

Row 2

Row 3

Figure 4

1 Following the instructions in Chapter 3, use the 3" (7.6cm) Fabric 1 squares and 4 of the 3" (7.6cm) Fabric 3 squares to make 8 Half-Square Triangles. Press the seams to the dark side and square each block to 2¼" (5.7cm).

2 Place 2 Half-Square Triangles right sides together, Fabric 1 on top of Fabric 1. Sew together with a ¼" (6mm) seam allowance. Press the seam toward Fabric 1. Repeat with the remaining half-square blocks to make 4 unit 1 pieces (**Figure 1**).

3 Repeat steps 1 and 2 using the 3" (7.6cm) Fabric 2 squares and the remaining 3" (7.6cm) Fabric 3 squares. You will have 4 unit 2 pieces (**Figure 2**).

4 Place 1 unit 1 on top of a unit 2, right sides together, aligning Fabric 3. Sew on the predominantly Fabric 2 edge with a ¼" (6mm) seam allowance. Press the block open and square to 4" (10.2cm) (**Figure 3**).

Repeat with the remaining unit 1 and unit 2 pieces. You will have 4 blocks.

5 Lay out the 4 blocks created in step 4 with the 4" (10.2cm) Fabric 1 square and the four 4" (10.2cm) Fabric 2 squares, using **Figure 4** as a guide.

TIP

ACCURATE CUTTING

Some of the best advice we can give beginners is to be as accurate as possible when cutting out your quilt block pieces. The more accurately you cut your pieces, the more professionally and precisely your quilt blocks will sew up. Three tools that will help you make precise cuts are a rotary cutter, a rotary ruler and a cutting mat (all of which can be purchased at your local quilting, craft or fabric store).

6 Assemble row 1 of the Ohio Star block by placing the second square of the row on top of the first square, right sides together. Stitch the right side seam with a ¼" (6mm) seam allowance and press the seam toward the darker fabric.

Join the third square to the second square in the same manner (**Figure 5**). Press the seam to the right.

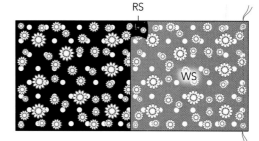

Figure 5

7 Sew the squares in rows 2 and 3 in the same way as described in step 6. Press row 2 to the left and row 3 to the right.

8 Join the 3 rows of the Ohio Star block. Start by placing the second row on top of the first, right sides together, and pin in place. Sew with a ¼" (6mm) seam allowance and press the seam open.

Join the third row to the second in the same manner. (**Figure 6**). Press the seam open. Square the block to 11" (27.9cm).

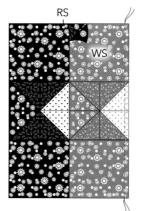

Figure 6

9 Place the 2½" × 11" (6.4cm × 27.9cm) strip along the bottom of the Ohio Star block, right sides together, and pin in place. Stitch with a ¼" (6mm) seam allowance. Press the seam toward the strip.

10 Place the 5" × 13" (12.7cm × 33cm) strip on the left side of the Ohio Star block, right sides together, and pin. Sew with a ¼" (6mm) seam allowance. Press the seam toward the dark side.

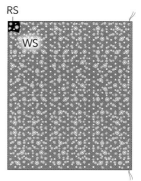

Figure 7

11 Place a 15½" (39.4cm) edge of the 15½" × 16½" (39.4cm × 41.9cm) strip along the top of the Ohio Star block, right sides together, and pin. Stitch with a ¼" (6mm) seam allowance (**Figure 7**) and press the seam toward the dark side.

12 Quilt and bind the cover following the directions in Chapter 1.

13 Measure 10" (25.4cm) up from the bottom of the cover along one long side and pin one end of one of the elastic pieces to the backside. Sew the end of the elastic into place.

Measure 10" (25.4cm) from the top of the cover and pin the other end of the elastic in place. Stitch to secure (**Figure 8**).

14 Repeat step 13 with the remaining piece of elastic on the other side of the cover. Press.

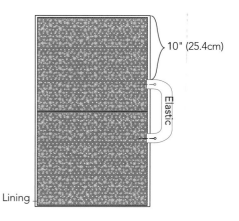

Figure 8

OHIO STAR QUILT

Finished Dimensions: 73" × 73" (185.4cm × 185.4cm)

MATERIALS

1¼ yards (1.1m) striped fabric (Fabric 1)

⅔ yard (0.6m) Swiss dot (Fabric 2)

½ yard (0.5m) red print fabric (Fabric 3)

½ yard (0.5m) floral lattice fabric (Fabric 4)

½ yard (0.5m) large floral on white fabric (Fabric 5)

½ yard (0.5m) small floral fabric (Fabric 6)

2⅛ yards (1.9m) large floral on black fabric (Fabric 7)

¾ yard (0.7m) white fabric (Fabric 8)

4½ yards (4.1m) of backing fabric

¾ yard (0.7m) of binding fabric

78" (198.1cm) square of batting

Walking foot (for sewing machine; optional)

Basting spray (optional)

Removable fabric marker (optional)

> *"After all, a woman didn't leave much behind in the world to show she'd been there. Even the children she bore and raised got their father's name. But her quilts, now that was something she could pass on."*
>
> —Sandra Dallas

CUTTING INSTRUCTIONS

Fabric 1 (striped)
Cut (72) 4½" (11.4cm) squares

Fabric 2 (Swiss dot)
Cut (36) 4½" (11.4cm) squares

Fabric 3 (red print)
Cut (8) 4½" (11.4cm) squares
Cut (2) 7½" (19.1cm) squares

Fabric 4 (floral lattice)
Cut (8) 4½" (11.4cm) squares
Cut (2) 7½" (19.1cm) squares

Fabric 5 (large floral on white)
Cut (8) 4½" (11.4cm) squares
Cut (2) 7½" (19.1cm) squares

Fabric 6 (small floral)
Cut (8) 4½" (11.4cm) squares
Cut (2) 7½" (19.1cm) squares

Fabric 7 (large floral on black)
Cut (4) 4½" (11.4cm) squares
Cut (1) 7½" (19.1cm) square
Cut (2) 63½" × 5" (161.3cm × 12.7cm) strips
Cut (2) 72½" × 5" (184.2cm × 12.7cm) strips

Fabric 8 (white)
Cut (36) 7½" (19.1cm) squares

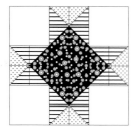

**Figure 1:
Blocks 1 and 9**

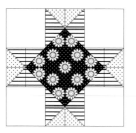

**Figure 3:
Blocks 3 and 7**

**Figure 2:
Blocks 2 and 8**

**Figure 4:
Blocks 4 and 6**

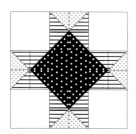

**Figure 5:
Block 5**

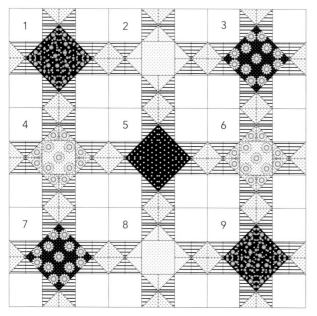

Quilt Top Diagram

1 Divide your fabric into the following groups and sew each group into Ohio Star blocks following the directions at the beginning of this chapter:

Group 1: (16) 4½" (11.4cm) Fabric 1 squares; (8) 4½" (11.4cm) Fabric 2 squares; (8) 4½" (11.4cm) and (2) 7½" (19.1cm) Fabric 3 squares; (8) 7½" (19.1cm) Fabric 8 squares. This group will make 2 complete Ohio Star blocks (**Figure 1**). Square each block to 21½" (54.6cm).

Group 2: (16) 4½" (11.4cm) Fabric 1 squares; (8) 4½" (11.4cm) Fabric 2 squares; (8) 4½" (11.4cm) and (2) 7½" (19.1cm) Fabric 4 squares; (8) 7½" (19.1cm) Fabric 8 squares. This group will make 2 complete Ohio Star blocks (**Figure 2**). Square each block to 21½" (54.6cm).

Group 3: (16) 4½" (11.4cm) Fabric 1 squares; (8) 4½" (11.4cm) Fabric 2 squares; (8) 4½" (11.4cm) and (2) 7½" (19.1cm) Fabric 5 squares; (8) 7½" (19.1cm) Fabric 8 squares. This group will make 2 complete Ohio Star blocks (**Figure 3**). Square each block to 21½" (54.6cm).

Group 4: (16) 4½" (11.4cm) Fabric 1 squares; (8) 4½" (11.4cm) Fabric 2 squares; (8) 4½" (11.4cm) and (2) 7½" (19.1cm) Fabric 6 squares; (8) 7½" (19.1cm) Fabric 8 squares. This group will make 2 complete Ohio Star blocks (**Figure 4**). Square each block to 21½" (54.6cm).

Group 5: (8) 4½" (11.4cm) Fabric 1 squares; (4) 4½" (11.4cm) Fabric 2 squares; (4) 4½" (11.4cm) and (1) 7½" (19.1cm) Fabric 7 squares; (4) 7½" (19.1cm) Fabric 8 squares. This group will make 1 complete Ohio Star block (**Figure 5**). Square the block to 21½" (54.6cm).

2 Lay out your quilt blocks using the Quilt Top Diagram.

3 Starting in row 1 of your quilt, place the second block of the row on top of the first block, right sides together. Stitch the right side seam with a ¼" (6mm) seam allowance and press the seam to one side; odd rows to the right, even rows to the left.

Join the third block to the second block in the same manner (**Figure 6**). Press the seam to one side; odd rows to the right, even rows to the left.

4 Repeat step 3 to assemble rows 2 and 3 of the quilt top.

5 Join the 3 rows. Start by placing the second row on top of the first, right sides together, and pin in place. Sew with a ¼" (6mm) seam allowance and press the seam open.

Join the third row to the second in the same manner. (**Figure 7**). Press the seam open.

6 Square your quilt top to 63½" (161.3cm) as described in Chapter 1.

7 Place a 63½" × 5" (161.3cm × 12.7cm) strip on the right side of the quilt top, right sides together. Align the right edges and pin. Sew the seam with a ¼" (6mm) seam allowance (**Figure 8**). Press the seam open.

Repeat on the other side of the quilt top, joining the second 63½" × 5" (161.3cm × 12.7cm) strip.

8 Place a 72½" × 5" (184.2cm × 12.7cm) strip on the top of the quilt top, right sides together. Align the top edges and pin. Sew the seam with a ¼" (6mm) seam allowance. Press the seam open.

Repeat on the bottom of the quilt top, joining the second 72½" × 5" (184.2cm × 12.7cm) strip.

9 Piece together a backing that is 81" (205.7cm) square following the directions in Chapter 1. If you plan on sending your quilt to a long-arm quilter, you're done!

10 If you're basting and quilting the quilt yourself, follow the methods described in Chapter 1.

11 Bind your quilt following the instructions in Chapter 1.

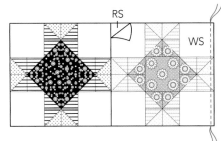

Figure 6

Figure 7

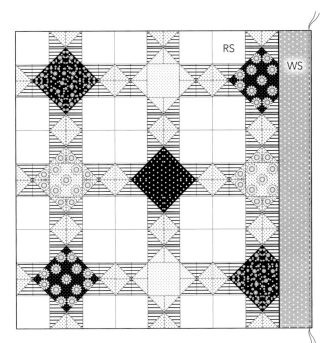

Figure 8

ABOUT THE AUTHORS

Elizabeth Evans

I learned to sew at a young age from women who loved the art. I owe so much to my maternal grandma, Lova (she always said her name was "love with an a"), who gave me a sewing machine for my twelveth birthday. I also owe so many of my sewing skills to a great Home Economics teacher who taught me not to fear the zipper or the buttonhole and let me sew whatever I wanted in class. What a gift that was! And finally, I owe my mom. She was a good mom, who was always crafting with her hands—whether it was sewing, crocheting, knitting or cross-stitching, she taught me the joys of handiwork.

And now as the mom of three, I hope to share that gift of sewing with not only my children but my posterity. I believe in the art of sewing, I believe in the power of creativity and I want them to know that. Sewing has brought me so much joy in my life, and I hope to be able to share the spark of sewing with them, and all of you.

liZ Evans

There once was a farmer's wife named Elizabeth Whitaker. She was an amazing cook, housekeeper, mother, and quilter. She also happened to be my great-grandmother, the one whom I am named after and a person who I spent the majority of my life thinking I had absolutely nothing in common with.

My name is liZ Evans. I like books, nachos, Disneyland, white t-shirts and art. I do not like rules, rodents, country music, or math. I also used to be strongly opposed to all things domestic until one day something happened that, like magic, changed my entire life in the twinkling of an eye.

That something was the birth of my son. When Simon was slipped into my arms, the one hundred years that separated my life from that of my great-grandmother's started to fall away and I knew that I wanted to become as amazing as her legend had become.

I'm not there yet. Nowhere close, of course. But I revel in my family. I absolutely love being a wife and a mother. I could (and do) spend hours cooking, cleaning, quilting and playing with my children. For me there is no place like home, especially if all my loved ones are here with me. I am thankful every day for the life I get to lead and for the chance I have to learn and love what my namesake understood so long ago.

TEMPLATES

Template pieces are shown at 50%. Enlarge to 200% to use.

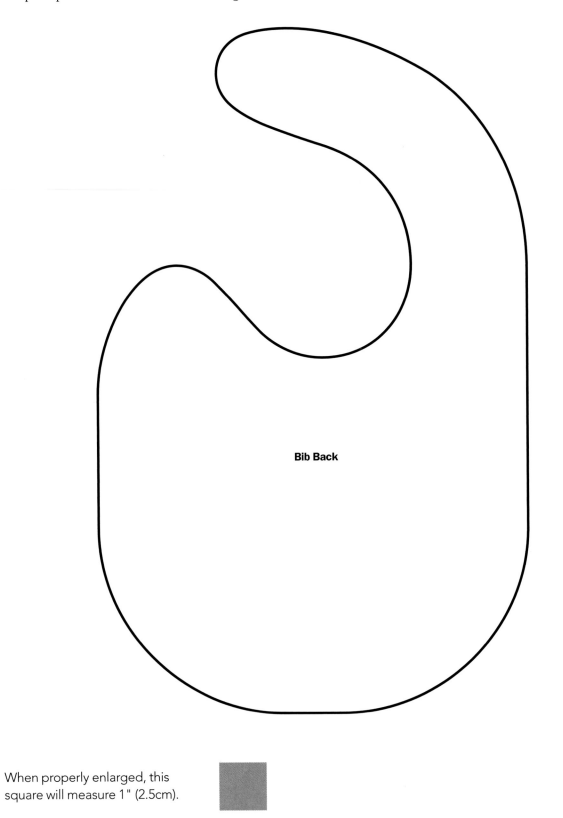

Bib Back

When properly enlarged, this
square will measure 1" (2.5cm).

TEMPLATES

Template pieces are shown at 50%. Enlarge to 200% to use.

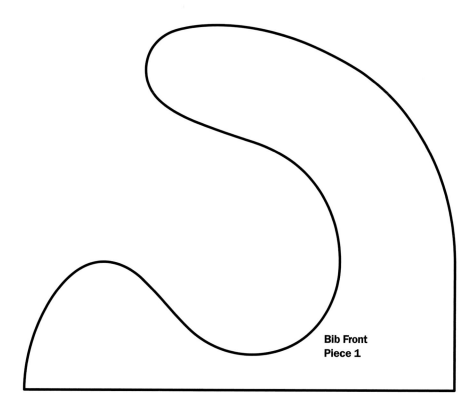

**Bib Front
Piece 1**

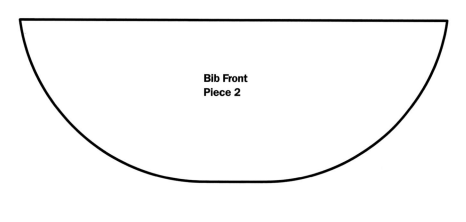

**Bib Front
Piece 2**

When properly enlarged, this
square will measure 1" (2.5cm).

GLOSSARY

Backstitch: A stitch used to secure sewing at the beginning and the end of a seam. Stitch forward 4–5 stitches, stitch backwards over where you just stitched, and then stitch forward again.

Baste: To sew temporarily by hand or by machine. This process in quilting is to hold the layers of fabric and batting together before the quilting process. Basting can be done through long stitches (hand or machine), quilting pins or spray bastes. (See Chapter 1 for more detail.)

Baste-stitch: Basting done by machine using the longest stitch length (sometimes referred to as *machine-baste*).

Batting: The soft layer of fiber placed between the quilt top and quilt backing. Batting can be made of cotton, silk, synthetic fibers or wool and comes in various thicknesses. Batting gives quilts their body and fullness.

Bias: The true diagonal of a square cloth.

Binding: A single or double fold of fabric that encases a raw edge as a finish or trim. Long, thin strips are sewn to the edge of the quilt to finish the edges. See Chapter 1 for more detail.

Block: The basic unit of a quilt. Blocks are usually square (but can be different shapes) and can be pieced, appliquéd or made up of a single fabric.

Borders: Strips of fabric that run around the edge of a quilt, often used to "frame" the quilt, unify the blocks or showcase the piecing. Borders can be any width.

Directional prints: Fabric that is printed with a definite top and bottom to the fabric.

Fat eighth: A quarter yard of fabric that is cut in half at the fold, measuring 9" × 22" (22.9cm × 55.9cm).

Fat quarter: A half yard of fabric that is cut in half at the fold, measuring 18" × 22" (45.7cm × 55.9cm).

Feed dogs: A mechanism below the presser foot in your sewing machine that moves the fabric through the machine as you stitch. The feed dogs need to be disabled if you are free-motion quilting.

Four-patch block: A quilt block made up of four pieces of fabric, usually sewn in two rows of two.

Free-motion quilting: The process of quilting the three layers of a quilt on a home sewing machine.

Free-motion quilting foot: A sewing machine presser foot that is used when the feed dogs are disengaged. A free-motion quilting foot can also be called a *hopper* or *darning foot*.

Gather: To draw into folds or puckers, usually done by pulling together machine- or hand-stitching.

Grain: The direction of threads in a woven fabric. The lengthwise grain runs parallel to the selvage edge. The crosswise grain runs from selvage to selvage. For professional-looking quilts, all grain lines should run in the same direction.

Hand quilting: The process of stitching together a quilt top, batting and quilt backing by hand. See Chapter 1 for more information.

Loft: Refers to the thickness of the batting in a quilt. The higher the loft, the thicker the batting. Keep in mind that a higher loft does not necessarily mean a warmer quilt.

Long-arm quilting: The process of using a long-arm sewing machine to quilt a quilt.

Miter: To sew fabric together at a 45° angle. Mitering is used on the corners of quilt binding. See Chapter 1 for more details.

Patchwork: Refers to the technique of sewing small pieces of fabric together to form patterns and designs and thereby creating a larger piece of fabric to be used on quilts, pillows, etc. Also known as *piecework*.

Piecing: Refers to the process of sewing fabrics together to form a quilt block.

Pin basting: Placing pins parallel with seam line in preparation for quilting.

Pinking: Jagged-cut finish for a raw edge to keep fabrics from fraying.

Pressing: The process of setting an iron on top of seam allowances to press them open or to the side.

Presser foot: Holds the fabric securely in place as the stitch is formed.

Quarter-inch foot: A presser foot for a sewing machine that has a ¼" (6mm) guide used for accuracy in piecing quilt blocks and quilt tops.

Quilt back: The bottom layer of a quilt, also called "backing." The backing is usually constructed of fabrics pieced to the size of the quilt top plus several inches to allow for shifting during the quilting process.

Quilt: Bed covering comprised of a top, padding and backing held together with stitching or ties.

Quilting: The process of securing the three components of a quilt together. Quilting can be done by hand or by machine with decorative or straight stitches. Quilting as a process traps air between the three layers, adding warmth to the finished quilt.

Quilt frame: A large floor frame that holds the three layers of a quilt secure so that the quilt can be hand quilted or tied.

Quilting hoop: A small circular hoop used in hand quilting to secure the three quilt layers.

Quilting ruler: Usually a plexiglass ruler with grid lines. It also has a grooved edge to guide a rotary cutter.

Quilt sandwich: Refers to the three layers: the quilt top facing up, the batting in the middle and the quilt backing facing down.

Quilt top: Refers to the top of the quilt.

Right side: The "front" side of a fabric.

Rotary cutter: A hand-held cutting tool with a round sharp blade used to roll along a quilting ruler to make straight cuts. Generally used with a rotary mat and quilting ruler.

Rotary mat: A cutting surface that is self healing. Generally used with a rotary cutter and quilting ruler.

Sashing: Strips of fabric that are sewn around or between quilt blocks.

Seam: The stitching line where two pieces of fabric are joined.

Seam allowance: Extra fabric allowed along the seams by the pattern. The standard quilting seam allowance is ¼" (6mm).

Seam Ripper: A tool used for cutting out or unpicking stitches.

Selvage: The finished border on the fabric.

Setting the seam: Placing your iron on the seam allowance before you press it open or to one side. It helps secure the threads before pressing the seam allowance into place.

Stitch length: Determines the distance the feed dogs move the fabric under the needle and presser foot. Stitch length will make your stitches longer or shorter.

Stitch-in-the-ditch: A quilting term used to describe the quilting process of stitching along patchwork seams in order to join the quilt top, the batting and the quilt backing.

Stitch width: Controls the needle swing from side to side on zigzag stitches. (And it will make your stitches wider or thinner.)

Strip piecing: A quilting technique where strips of fabric are cut and sewn together. The quilt blocks are later cut from these "strips." *Rail Fence* quilts as well as others use strip piecing.

Tension: Correct tension ensures that the same amount of thread flows from both the spool and the bobbin simultaneously to form a neat, tidy interlocking stitch.

Topstitching: A line of stitching along the seam line on the right side of the garment or quilt to add strength or design.

Walking foot: A presser foot attachment that allows sewing through thicker layers.

Wrong side: The "back" side of a fabric.

INDEX

ACKNOWLEDGMENTS

Many thanks to the following companies for their help with this book:
baby lock
Kelly Crawford
Michael Miller Fabrics
Riley Blake Fabrics
Westminster Fabrics
Andover Fabrics
Sew Shabby Quilting

fw

a content + ecommerce company

www.fwcommunity.com

20 19 18 17 16   5 4 3 2 1

Distributed in Canada by Fraser Direct
100 Armstrong Avenue
Georgetown, ON, Canada L7G 5S4
Tel: (905) 877-4411

Distributed in the U.K. and Europe by
F&W MEDIA INTERNATIONAL
Brunel House, Newton Abbot, Devon, TQ12 4PU, England
Tel: (+44) 1626 323200, Fax: (+44) 1626 323319
E-mail: enquiries@fwmedia.com

Distributed in Australia by Capricorn Link
P.O. Box 704, S. Windsor NSW, 2756 Australia
Tel: (02) 4560 1600, Fax: (02) 4577 5288
E-mail: books@capricornlink.com.au

SRN: S3158
ISBN-13: 978-1-4402-4544-2

Edited by Stephanie White
Designed by Laura Spencer
Production coordinated by Jennifer Bass
Photography by liZ and Elizabeth Evans
Illustrations by Sue Friend

Any available errata can be found at www.quiltingdaily.com/errata

DEDICATION

We have a lot in common: the same number of children, the same age, the same great educations, the same in-laws and of course the same name. But we also have something else in common: loyal husbands, wonderful children and loving parents. And it is to that endearing group of people that we dedicate this book. We love you with all of our hearts.

METRIC CONVERSION CHART

TO CONVERT:	TO:	MULTIPLY BY:
inches	centimeters	2.54
centimeters	inches	0.4
feet	centimeters	30.5
centimeters	feet	0.03
yards	meters	0.9
meters	yards	1.1

KEEP QUILTING WITH FONS & PORTER!

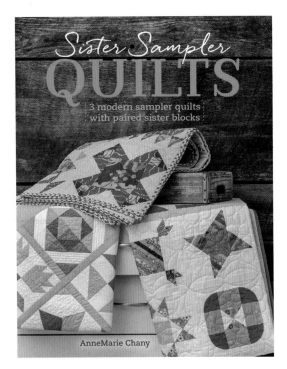

Sister Sampler Quilts
AnneMarie Chany
ISBN: 978-1-4402-4503-9
$19.99

Dear Quilty
Mary Fons
ISBN: 978-1-4402-4318-9
$22.99

Do you love quilting but want a more modern aesthetic? If so, you'll love *Sister Sampler Quilts*. Inside, you'll find 25 interchangeable sister blocks and 3 sampler quilts that challenge traditional grid layouts with fun, innovative settings. Create block pairs as identical sisters or flip flop the color schemes for a patchier appeal in quilts that beautifully bridge the gap between traditional and modern. Whether you're a beginner or a more advanced quilter, you'll enjoy practicing and perfecting quilting basics, such as half-square triangles, flying geese and hourglass blocks, to beautiful effect.

Pulled from the pages of *Quilty* magazine, this collection of 12 beginner-friendly quilts has everything you love about the magazine: straightforward instructions, helpful hints, and a sense of humor. Go behind the scenes to learn about the people who make *Quilty* possible and get to know the designers of your favorite quilts. Whether you're a complete quilting newbie or have several quilts under your belt, *Dear Quilty* is here to help, every stitch of the way.

QuiltingDaily

For nearly a decade, Quilting Daily has been the place to learn, be inspired and enjoy other quilters just like you. We bring you expert advice from our magazine editors, book editors, and Cate Prato, the editor of Quilting Daily.